Coming Out Of the Dark

A Child's Stolen Innocence

To the child abusers and predators of the world.

Just remember we grow up and we will have a voice.

Joseph Christensen

To every survivor who has whispered their truth into the darkness, may this story be a beacon of hope, illuminating the path towards healing and a life reclaimed.

This book is dedicated to the courageous souls who have fought tirelessly to overcome unimaginable adversity, to the children whose innocence has been stolen, but whose spirits remain unbroken.

It is a testament to the enduring power of the human spirit, to the unwavering belief in the possibility of a brighter future, even after the darkest of nights. It is for those who have sought solace in the silence, and for those who are finally finding their voice to tell their own story, your strength inspires me every single day.

To my therapists, counselors, friends, and family who believed in my recovery when I couldn't believe in myself: thank you. Your support has been the lifeline I desperately needed during the toughest times, providing solace and encouragement along the journey to healing.

To every individual in the world who offers a helping hand, a kind word, or a listening ear, know that your compassion helps mend shattered hearts and makes the world a better place, one act of kindness at a time. To those still in the darkness or in denial of their trauma, know you are not alone, healing is possible, and you will have the strength to overcome this and raise your voice against the predators.

There is hope.

Acknowledgements

Writing this book only touches on a small part of my early childhood. Honestly, I could write a second book, but this has been a deeply personal and challenging journey, one that I could not have undertaken without the unwavering support of many incredible individuals for without them in my life, I would not be here today.

First and foremost, I want to thank my dearest friend Brian. Your guidance, love and friendship throughout my life, even today, are irreplaceable and so precious to me. I am who I am because you saw a better life for me and guided me and without that I would not be here.

I am especially grateful to my son Marcus for his unknown support and strength that he gives me just by being himself and for his hugs, his help, his laughter and those silly jokes. One day he will understand I am overprotective of him for a reason. I just want to protect him from the dangers out there until he is old enough to understand and navigate the world as a man. It will never stop me worrying about him.

Most importantly, to my family, my mum, for without her and her approval, this book would not have been written, and to Timmy, Ariel, and Matthew, who all offered unconditional love even after years of silence on my part and for understanding, offering a safe space for me to process things, knowing I was not ok even when I said I was. Everyone's unwavering belief in my ability to heal and their unwavering support really did give me the courage to share my story and bare my soul to the world.

My gratitude extends to my friends Meryl, Mark, Brian, Jillian, Adam, Scott, Kel, Sarah and Crystle for all their unwavering support and guidance.

To my therapists, whose guidance, patience, and unwavering belief in my strength were instrumental in my healing process. Their expertise and compassionate support provided the bedrock upon which I was able to build a new life and step out of the darkness with my head held high.

I also wish to acknowledge and thank Brian and Mark for being the first eyes over my draft and for their genuine, heartfelt support.

I would like to thank my official editors, Books Publishing Company at 2425 West Loop South, Huston, Texas 77027, USA, for their meticulous work and insightful guidance. Their sensitivity was essential in ensuring that my story was told with both honesty and respect.

Contents

Preface

Writing this book has been both a cathartic release of raw emotion and terrifying. For years, the memories I share within these pages were locked away, buried deep beneath layers of shame, fear, and self-doubt. To confront them, to articulate them, to give them form and voice felt like opening a deep wound that had never fully healed. Yet, in the process of writing, I discovered something extraordinary: the power of narrative to transform trauma into testimony, to convert pain into purpose.

This book is not just my story; it is a testament to the resilience of the human spirit. It's a testament to the hope that can bloom even in the most desolate landscapes of the soul. I share my graphic, detailed and raw experiences not to elicit pity or to dwell on the darkness of my past but to offer a light, a spark, a glimmer of hope to others who may be navigating similar struggles. I aim to provide validation, understanding and hope to you through my journey. I hope my story will demonstrate that healing is possible, that even after enduring unimaginable adversity, it is possible to find peace and purpose to reclaim your life and come out of the darkness.

My hope is that this book serves as a tool for empathy, understanding, and fostering open conversations about childhood trauma and abuse and the vital importance of creating safe and supportive environments for children everywhere. I hope this book validates the experiences of others, helps to reduce the stigma associated with abuse and trauma, and provides encouragement to those seeking help and recovery.

The journey to healing is long and often arduous, but it's a journey worth taking. Stand up, raise your voice from those dark places within and scream or whisper to yourself, but raise your voice to simply be heard by someone or even just to be heard aloud to yourself—I am worthy, I didn't cause this, I am not at fault, and I will come out the other side of this stronger.

Remember, YOU are not alone.

Introduction

My story begins in the harsh realities of a small city in far north Queensland called Townsville, a small coastal military town in Australia. Townsville is a city that holds both the painful memories of my childhood, sexual abuse and the seeds of my eventual recovery.

I was born prematurely to a young teenage mother struggling with her own demons. My early life was anything but idyllic. Poverty, instability, and neglect were constant companions. My mother's struggles, compounded by my absent father, created a chaotic and unpredictable environment that left me feeling vulnerable and alone.

The lack of stability, constant moves, and the precariousness of our living situations created an overwhelming sense of insecurity that impacted every aspect of my life. I witnessed domestic violence, financial struggles, and homelessness far beyond the comprehension of a young child.

Yet, these early hardships are not the entirety of my story. The most damaging wounds I carry are those inflicted through repeated sexual abuse starting at the tender age of seven. These graphic and traumatic experiences are the central focus of this book. I will detail the assaults, not to shock or sensationalise, but to shed light on the insidious nature of repeated abuse, the ways in which perpetrators manipulate and groom their victims, and the profound and lasting impact this has on a child's development.

More than just graphic accounts of abuse, this book charts a course through the darkness, illuminating the difficult journey toward healing, forgiveness, and self-acceptance. It is a journey fraught with challenges and moments of profound despair, yet ultimately characterised by hope and resilience.

I share my story with the hope of providing comfort to other survivors, offering insight to those who care about them, and raising awareness about a pervasive societal problem. This book is a testament to the strength of the human spirit, a reminder that even in the face of unimaginable adversity, healing and happiness are possible.

Premature Birth and Early Instability

My arrival into this world was anything but serene. Born 3.5 months premature, a tiny, fragile being that came and left the world several times, I entered a life already teetering on the edge of chaos. Being kept in hospital for over 6 months before being allowed to go home.

My mother, barely a woman herself, was a young teenager, only just 17 when I was born, grappling with the overwhelming burden of motherhood, a fractured family life compounded by her own undiagnosed mental health struggles from abuse. There was no loving partner to share the weight, no stable family network to offer support. Just her elderly mother and a young, overwhelmed woman facing an uncertain future and a baby who was not meant to survive and would become the unwitting casualty of her battles.

The lack of support systems around my mother and the absence of a strong, consistent parental figure were the invisible foundations upon which my early life would be built—a foundation of instability and insecurity.

The first few years were a blur of fleeting memories, fragmented images of cramped apartments and houses, the constant shifting of locations from Queensland through to Victoria, and the ever-present hum of anxiety that permeated every aspect of my existence. Townsville, my birthplace, became synonymous with this unsettling uncertainty.

We moved frequently, sometimes within the same city, other times to entirely different neighborhoods, each move reflecting my mother's struggle to find stability, both financially and emotionally. The places we lived in were never spacious, always crowded, and often shared with other families or extended relatives, a constant reminder of our precarious economic circumstances.

The spaces we called "home" were usually far from ideal, characterised by peeling paint, leaky faucets, and the ever-present scent of dampness and stale cigarette smoke. These weren't just physical descriptions; they were reflections of the instability that defined our lives. The lack of personal space, the constant noise and movement contributed to an overwhelming sense of chaos and unease that I felt profoundly. However, I couldn't articulate it at the time.

The anxiety that permeated our lives was tangible. It wasn't just the worry about money, though that was a constant companion. It was the unpredictable nature of my mother's moods, the abrupt changes in plans, the constant fear of eviction or moving again, and the ever-present threat of homelessness and danger that hung over us like a dark cloud. Even simple things like knowing where our next meal would come from or whether we would have a roof over our heads the following night became sources of deep-seated anxiety.

As a young child, I was acutely aware of this instability, the constant shifting sands beneath my feet, leaving me feeling insecure, vulnerable, and deeply alone. My early memories are replete with sensory details: the scratchy feel of cheap carpets or concrete floors we would sleep on, the smell of kerosene heaters, the bullet holes in the housing commission windows and the pungent smell from the communal rubbish, the bitter taste of instant noodles or rice a riso that formed the backbone of our diet.

Finding the brake lines were cut in the car or all 4 tires were slashed, having men stand outside your mother's window with rifles or knocking on the windows to try and coerce you out into the dark or waking to hear people running across the roof and banging on the front door, these seem absurd, but it's the truth.

These experiences weren't just details; they were visceral reminders of our poverty. They were the physical manifestations of our lack of resources, our inability to provide even the most basic comforts or safety nets.

This poverty wasn't simply a lack of money; it was a pervasive condition that permeated every aspect of our lives, shaping my worldview and influencing my developing sense of self.

The constant struggle for survival meant that my childhood was stripped of much of the simple joys, security and normalcy that most children take for granted.

The constant moving meant I never had a chance to form lasting friendships. I was always the 'new kid,' the outsider, perpetually on the fringe, never quite belonging. This sense of isolation, of being different, was profound and deeply unsettling. I felt like a nomad, always on the move, never settling anywhere long enough to establish roots to build meaningful connections.

This constant displacement had a profound effect on my sense of self and my identity, making me feel adrift, insecure, and uncertain of my place in the world. The lack of permanence in my life mirrored the instability within my own being; I felt as rootless and unstable as the shifting sands beneath my feet.

Furthermore, the financial hardships forced me to grow up too quickly. I was exposed to the adult world far earlier than any child should be. I witnessed arguments and sometimes even violence between my mother and her various partners.

The emotional fallout from these conflicts was intense, leaving a lasting impact on my psyche. I was a silent observer, privy to the undercurrents of emotional turmoil that often threatened to consume our lives. I learned to become acutely aware of adult anxieties, absorbing them like a sponge, internalising the constant fear and uncertainty as a part of my own being.

This premature exposure to the complexities of the adult world, a world characterised by conflict, instability and hardship, overshadowed my childhood, forever etching its mark on my soul. The struggles to make ends meet, the fear of hunger, the constant uncertainty about our housing and security–these were not simply background noise but the very soundtrack of my early existence.

My mother's bisexuality, while not overtly problematic in itself, added another layer of complexity to our already chaotic lives. It exposed me to a world of relationships and sexualities that I was far too young to understand. My understanding of sexuality was formed within the context of my mother's relationships, often turbulent and short-lived, frequently involving adults from the LGBTQIA+ community, known then as the gay scene.

This early exposure to the gay scene introduced a level of confusion and lack of clarity about human relationships, especially regarding sexual identity, that I grappled with for many years. The conversations I overheard and the interactions I witnessed often lacked the context and age-appropriateness necessary for a child to process.

These were adult conversations, adult experiences, presented to me within the framework of family life, which left me confused, unsure of what was normal, and acutely aware of the adult world's complexity far beyond my years. The combination of economic hardship, lack of stability and early exposure to adult relationships contributed to an unstable and confusing childhood.

Even within this instability, there were periods of relative calm, periods of love and stability. Still, they were just moments of connection, fleeting glimpses of what a normal childhood might look like. But these were rare oases in the vast, harsh desert of my reality. Some of the memories remain fragmented and fleeting, like half-remembered dreams–a comforting hug, a shared laugh, a moment of genuine connection that provided a brief respite from the pervasive anxiety. These moments, though precious and few, served as small beacons of hope, reminders that despite the overwhelming chaos, there was still some capacity for love and connection, however fragile and fleeting.

They also served as a painful counterpoint to the predominantly difficult experiences, fueling a deep longing for the stability and normalcy I desperately craved. The contrast between these rare moments of warmth and the overwhelming harshness of my daily life only served to intensify the feeling of deprivation and instability.

The absence of a consistent father figure further exacerbated the instability of my early years. His lack of presence due to having another partner and other children and also being 15 years older than my mother was a void that permeated my life. My father was replaced with my mother's partners, in many cases female who openly disliked men.

This lack of a consistent male role model, I believe, contributed significantly to my developing sense of insecurity and vulnerability. The absence of a stable father figure, coupled with my mother's struggles, created a vacuum that would be filled by other, often harmful, influences later in my life.

The lack of a stable male role model, no matter how butch my mother's girlfriends were, meant that I missed out on crucial aspects of a healthy male-female dynamic, leaving me ill-equipped to navigate future relationships, leading to an imbalance in my understanding of healthy boundaries and interactions between genders.

The unstable environment, coupled with my premature birth and my mother's mental health issues, meant that my early developmental years were far from typical. The lack of consistent care, the constant moving, and the pervasive sense of insecurity had a profound and lasting effect on my emotional and psychological development.

My early years weren't just chaotic; they laid the groundwork for the trauma that would follow, shaping my perception of the world, of myself, and my capacity to form healthy relationships. The seeds of instability sown in my infancy would sprout into the thorny realities of my later childhood.

We would often go into emergency housing, placed with a relative or friend of my mother for months due to her attempted suicide by cutting her wrists and being sanctioned into the psychiatric ward for months. Otherwise, we would relocate to another town due to the many dangers in our lives from men standing outside our windows at night with rifles to a man tapping on my sister's window, wanting to get in. People would run across the roof of the house at night, being followed home from school by cars and chased through drain ways or discovering someone had cut the brakes of the car. It certainly was not a normal life for a child.

We would often get up in the morning and go to school as normal and walk home to see the car loaded up with the bare basics and the house would be empty. Mum would say we are going on a trip then we would start from somewhere else and never go back to our previous place.

I remember moving to Victoria and sleeping on the floor in an empty house for weeks in a sleeping bag. My comfort was colouring books. I had to focus my mind on normality or a small white telescope and then, a few weeks later, observe two men bash a door down at night and threaten to kneecap them if they didn't pay up. Needless to say, within a day, we would do a midnight flit, and it would happen all over again.

Poverty and Exposure to the Adult World

Poverty wasn't a distant concept; it was the air we breathed, the clothes we wore, the gnawing hunger that often accompanied our meager meals. We moved frequently, a nomadic existence dictated by the ever-present threat of eviction.

Our homes were rarely more than cramped, dilapidated apartments, often in the less desirable parts of Townsville. The walls were thin, the sounds of our neighbors–their arguments, their laughter, their late-night activities–seeping into our lives. There was a constant undercurrent of anxiety, a pervasive feeling that we were always on the brink of losing everything. This instability, this constant state of precariousness, was deeply unsettling, creating a sense of unease and insecurity that clung to me like a second skin.

The lack of money meant a lack of choice. Our clothes were hand-me-downs, often patched and mended, a constant reminder of our financial struggles. Food was a constant concern. We often went without, resorting to whatever scraps we could find. But mum would always feed us children before she would eat and many nights, I remember her saying she wasn't hungry and it didn't register that it was because there was not enough food for everyone. The memory of empty shelves in the refrigerator, or just eating a carrot, a tomato or a pickled onion for lunch, and the gnawing hunger in my stomach are etched into my memory as vividly as if they were happening yesterday. This constant hunger wasn't just about the lack of food; it was a symbol of our overall lack of security, a constant reminder of our vulnerability. It shaped my perception of the world, coloring it with the hues of scarcity and deprivation.

Beyond the material deprivation, poverty exposed me to a harsh reality far beyond the understanding of a child. I witnessed the brutal realities of domestic violence, not as something I saw on television but as something that occurred within the confines of our own home.

The shouting, the crashing sounds of furniture being thrown, doors being kicked in, the fear etched on my mother's face the bruises and blood in the aftermath—these became the soundtrack to my early years. These weren't abstract concepts; they were visceral, terrifying experiences that left an indelible mark on my psyche. The volatility of our living situation fostered a deep-seated fear, a constant expectation of the next explosion, the next crisis.

The financial instability extended beyond our home life, impacting every aspect of my existence. I was acutely aware of the constant struggle to make ends meet, the strained conversations about overdue bills, borrowed money or sending me on 5km walks to borrow food from friends or relatives and the constant threat of homelessness. The knowledge of adults looking at fully furnished rentals getting a key cut and going back later, stealing and selling the furniture for cash or the conversations of trying to steal money from a known acquaintance late at night by assaulting them from behind in the dark.

I remember the shame associated not only with the knowledge of such issues but also with not having the same basics as other children, the feeling of being different, of being less than resonated deeply. This pervasive shame, the internalised sense of inadequacy, would later manifest in various ways, impacting my self-esteem and my ability to form healthy relationships.

My mother's bisexuality, while not directly related to poverty, was inextricably woven into the fabric of our financial struggles. Her relationships, often unstable and short-lived, brought with them their own unique set of challenges. The constant coming and going of different partners, each with their own personalities and demands, contributed to the feeling of instability and unpredictability that permeated my childhood.

The adult world, with all its complexities and anxieties, was thrust upon me prematurely, its harsh realities blurring the lines between childhood innocence and the cruel realities of survival. I was privy to conversations, arguments, and situations far beyond my comprehension, forced to navigate a world where adult concerns were the norm.

It wasn't just the fights or financial difficulties that exposed me to the adult world. My mother's involvement in the gay scene—a world both exciting and bewildering to me—provided an early glimpse into a facet of adult life that was simultaneously intriguing and terrifying. The bars, clubs and gatherings were strange and chaotic places, filled with people who were often inebriated or high on drugs, a stark contrast to the sheltered innocence that is normally associated with childhood.

I remember the bright lights, the loud music, the smoky atmosphere, and the intoxicating mixture of scents–perfumes, sweat, and alcohol. This wasn't the Disney version of adulthood; it was a chaotic, often disturbing reality that forced me to grow up too fast. I was privy to conversations about sex, relationships and finances, topics I was certainly not ready for and topics that were often sexually suggestive and, at times, explicitly sexual, causing significant confusion and anxiety.

The adult world I encountered wasn't just sexually charged; it was also deeply flawed and frequently dangerous. It was a world where vulnerability was often exploited, where boundaries were fluid and often disregarded, and where people used one another for personal gain or momentary gratification. It was a world devoid of the safety nets and protections that are supposed to safeguard children. It was purely the LGBTQIA+ community taking advantage of one another in any way they could. I saw desperation and loneliness and witnessed firsthand the human capacity for more deliberate, cold and calculated cruelty than compassion.

This constant exposure to the underbelly of society within the LGBTQIA+ community left me feeling vulnerable, scared and confused. I remember feeling that nobody really cared and nobody was looking out for me or other vulnerable children in those settings. It was a take-what-you-want world, a dog-eat-dog world, a bite-or-be-bitten world that I was forced to navigate from an incredibly young age.

Poverty wasn't just about a lack of material possessions; it was a pervasive state of being an ingrained sense of insecurity that affected every aspect of my life. It was the constant fear of eviction, the worry about where our next meal would come from, the anxiety associated with my mother's volatile moods, especially with my sister, and the overwhelming sense of being lost and alone in a world that seemed determined to break me.

It wasn't just a matter of survival; it was a matter of emotional and psychological survival. It created a deep-seated sense of powerlessness, a feeling that I had no control over my life or my destiny. This pervasive sense of powerlessness would become a recurring theme throughout my life.

The consequences of this early exposure to the adult world were profound and far-reaching. My childhood wasn't a time of innocence and carefree play; it was a period of constant vigilance, of trying to protect myself from the dangers that lurked around every corner. The world was not a safe place, not for me. It was a place where adults were unreliable, where violence was commonplace, and where my own body was at risk.

My sense of security and well-being was shattered, replaced by a deep-seated fear that would color my perception of the world for years to come. This fear extended beyond just the physical dangers to encompass a more pervasive sense of unease and anxiety, an ever-present feeling of being unsafe and unprotected.

The experiences of my childhood, shaped by poverty and exposure to the adult world, were formative and deeply traumatic. They echo in the corners of my mind even today, yet I tell myself I will not become that, I will not that define me, I will be so much more.

As a child, they profoundly affected my development, impacting my self-esteem, my ability to form healthy relationships and my overall sense of well-being. However, they did not define me. Despite the hardships and the trauma, I survived. My story is a testament to the resilience of the human spirit, a testament to the incredible ability of a child and, ultimately, a person to find hope and healing amidst the darkest of times.

That journey of healing—of reclaiming my life, is a story for another chapter. But this part of my story, the foundational layers of poverty and early exposure to the harsh realities of the adult world, is essential to understanding the scars that needed healing and the strength it took to overcome them.

The experiences ingrained a survival instinct into me, hypervigilance and awareness of my surroundings and the people in them. These became the tools I used to navigate the treacherous landscape of my early years, to try and maintain control when I felt most out of control.

Introduction to the Gay Scene

My mother's bisexuality wasn't something she discussed. It was well-known and simply a facet of her life, as visible and unavoidable as the overflowing ashtrays or the persistent smell of cheap cigarettes that clung to our clothes.

Her relationships were a kaleidoscope of fleeting connections, a whirlwind of personalities that swirled through our lives, leaving behind a residue of emotional instability and uncertainty. Most were women, some were men, and the lines between casual acquaintances and more intimate relationships often blurred, leaving me utterly confused and disoriented and yearning for the loss of friendships, love and connection I had formed with some of these people.

I remember the women—a succession of faces, names fading into the hazy backdrop of my early memories. Kristine, a beautiful woman with fiery red hair who smelled of lavender, a firm and kind woman her laughter loud and echoing, another mother figure and role model to me. The quiet sadness of her departure quickly replaced the brightness and joy she instilled in our family.

Stephanie, a stunning blonde woman with beautiful hair, drove a panel van, and boy, she had a smile that lit up a room.

However, her eyes were perpetually shadowed with sadness. She was with us for a long time. Stephanie was another mother and role model to me, a fun woman who brought happiness and joy to our lives in many ways, but she, like the others, faded from our lives. Stephanie's absence left me feeling a deep loss, a sense of emptiness and lack of closure, a subtle tension that ran beneath the surface of all my mother's relationships.

Kay, a stunning blonde, a silver lady with long, straight hair and pale skin, who I adored but she lived in Victoria.

Cheryl, a masculine brunette who wore Brut33 and Blue Stratos aftershaves, lived with us in a house in a suburb called North Ward. I did have a bit of a crush on her, but again, another relationship ended, leaving me feeling a sense of loss and abandonment.

Biddy, a lovely strong woman with chestnut curls that loved horses and worked at the supermarket, lived with us in a suburb called Rupertswood, she gave us a good life and we all loved her like a second mother. She was cherished deeply, and I still miss her to this day.

All these strong and venerable women were guiding lights in my life, and I still cherish all my memories of them and I always will.

These women were so very different from the men—the men who would come and go, their presence often marked by a heavy silence or a tense energy that made the air crackle with unspoken anxieties.

Keep in mind the Gay Scene I refer to was all-inclusive, but back then, it was just called the gay scene as it was lesbians and gays. Yes, there were many bisexuals and transgenders in the community, but it was always referred to simply as the gay scene. The LGB reference only came in later years and now it's referred to as the LGBTQIA+ community.

The gay scene in Townsville, as I experienced it through my mother's life, wasn't the glamorous portrayal often presented in media. It was raw, unfiltered, dangerous and often unsettling.

It was a world of dimly lit pubs, regular bar fights over who owned who or who was sleeping with who, smokey bars, and clandestine meetings in back alleys–places where I, as a child, felt perpetually out of place, yet acutely aware and often watching from the back seat of the car. I wasn't an active participant, of course, but I was a silent observer, a witness to interactions that were far beyond my comprehension.

I saw affection, but I also saw conflict, violence, jealousy, and a vulnerability that was both captivating and frightening. The adults around me, in their attempts to navigate their own complex emotions and identities, often failed to consider my perspective, my innocence, and the impact of their actions on a young, impressionable child. Their world, with its fluidity of relationships and exploration of sexuality, was jarringly different from the sheltered world I was supposed to inhabit.

It was a world where boundaries were often blurred, and my own sense of safety felt precarious and constantly shifting. I learned early on that intimacy didn't always mean affection and that touch didn't always equal care.

The casual nature of some of these interactions, the frequent comings and goings, left me feeling adrift. I longed for stability, for the consistency of a loving, predictable family life, a longing that was perpetually unmet. The instability of my mother's relationship directly impacted my sense of security and belonging. My understanding of love, family, and relationships was fundamentally warped by this early exposure to a world of adult complexities.

One specific memory stands out, though the details are hazy with the passage of time. I recall a night in a smoky bar, the air thick with cigarette smoke and the murmur of conversations. My mother was talking to a group of people, their laughter loud against the background music at the Seaview Hotel.

I was tucked away in a corner with a lemonade and raspberry drink and some pork crackle, quietly playing Pac-Man, trying to find some sense of normalcy in the chaotic environment. Suddenly, a hand reached out and touched my leg. It wasn't a kind touch; it was intrusive, unsettling. I looked up, but I couldn't discern who it was in the dim light.

The brief moment of discomfort was quickly dismissed in the chaos surrounding me, but it left an imprint, a subtle unease that added to the growing collection of anxieties that shaped my childhood.

Another incident, much, much clearer in my memory, involved a man named Robert. He became a frequent visitor when we lived in Hermit Park a rundown suburb of Townsville, as it was a smelly suburb and near the refuse tip.

I remember the mirrored walls and the duckling I came home with one day. There was a party. Mum and her partner had the metal drums of seafood as Mum's partner worked down at the wharf in the seafood area and I always liked her big-white gumboots that she used for work.

Robert was kind and a friend of my mums, offering me treats and engaging me in childish games, but there was a peculiar intimacy to his interactions, a level of closeness that felt uncomfortable. His touch, while not overtly abusive, was far too familiar, too intimate for a child. It was an insidious form of boundary violation, leaving me feeling confused and unable to articulate what was wrong. This blurred line between acceptable affection and predatory behavior is something I have struggled with long after those early experiences.

These early experiences didn't just impact my understanding of sexuality; they profoundly shaped my self-esteem and self-worth.

Growing up in this environment, where the boundaries between platonic friendship, casual intimacy, and something more were constantly shifting, created a deep sense of confusion and uncertainty within me. I struggled to distinguish between affection and exploitation. I couldn't fully comprehend the complexities of adult relationships, and I felt a constant pressure to be older, to understand more than a child should have to.

This premature exposure to the adult world, especially the complexities of sexuality, affected my ability to form healthy relationships. I developed an acute awareness of my vulnerability, a hypervigilance that became both a survival mechanism and a source of chronic anxiety. I struggled to trust adults, and I often felt a deep sense of isolation, disconnected from my peers who seemed to inhabit a different, less turbulent reality.

Navigating the gay scene through the lens of a traumatised child was particularly challenging. I often felt like an outsider looking in, unable to fully understand or participate in the dynamics I was witnessing. The adults in this world, often grappling with their own identities and struggles, were ill-equipped to protect me from the inherent risks.

Their own experiences of marginalisation didn't translate into empathy for my vulnerability. The lack of education surrounding consent and healthy boundaries was another crucial factor.

Children need clear and consistent instructions on what constitutes appropriate behavior and how to protect themselves from abuse. This education was entirely missing from my life, leaving me vulnerable to exploitation and emotional harm. The absence of safe adults who could offer guidance and support compounded the trauma of my early experiences.

In reflecting on these early years, I see a clear connection between my mother's lifestyle and the challenges I faced. Her bisexuality itself was not inherently problematic; the issue stemmed from the lack of stability and the inherent risks associated with her transient relationships and the people she allowed into our lives.

The instability of our living situation, the poverty we experienced, and the lack of parental guidance all played significant roles in the trauma I endured. It's crucial to acknowledge that not all children raised in similar circumstances will experience the same level of trauma. Resilience, access to support networks, and individual coping mechanisms all play a vital role.

However, my experience highlights the potential vulnerabilities of children exposed to complex family dynamics, especially in the absence of sufficient protection and guidance.

My journey to healing involved confronting these early experiences, accepting the lasting impact they had on my life, and learning to navigate the world with a newfound understanding of myself and my boundaries. It was a long and difficult path, but it was a journey that ultimately led to resilience and a renewed sense of hope.

The path to healing wasn't linear; it was a winding road with many detours and setbacks. But with each step forward, I gained a stronger sense of self-awareness and a deeper understanding of my own strength and resilience. This understanding is what I hope to convey through my story.

The fact that I survived, that I found the strength to heal, and that I am now able to share my story is a testament to the inherent resilience of the human spirit. This is not just my story; it is a story about the importance of recognising and addressing the vulnerabilities of children and the vital need for creating a supportive environment where healing and recovery are possible.

Early Signs of Abuse and Neglect

The earliest memories aren't sharp photographs — they are more like faded watercolors, smudged and indistinct. Fragments of sensation, snippets of emotion, cling to the edges of my consciousness. The dominant feeling is one of pervasive insecurity, a constant low hum of anxiety that permeated every aspect of my early life. It wasn't a single, dramatic event that defined my childhood's instability, but rather a gradual erosion of safety and security, a slow drip of neglect that wore away at my sense of self.

My mother, young and overwhelmed, struggled to provide even the most basic of necessities. Food was often scarce, and meals were irregular and inconsistent. Sometimes, there was nothing at all, and the gnawing emptiness in my stomach mirrored the hollowness I felt inside. It wasn't malicious neglect; it was born of her own struggles with mental health, a relentless cycle of depression and instability that swallowed her whole, leaving little room for the needs of a premature infant.

We lived hand-to-mouth, constantly moving from one cramped, inadequate dwelling to another, each move a jarring disruption to any sense of normalcy a child might crave. The constant shifting of landscapes mirrored the instability in our lives—a precarious existence where stability was an elusive dream.

Sleep was fragmented and often disturbed. The constant shifting of environments and the transient nature of our living situations meant that finding a stable place to rest my head was a perpetual challenge. The rooms we inhabited were rarely clean or comfortable, and the sounds of the adult world–arguments, shouting, the slamming of doors–frequently intruded on my fragile sleep.

These sleepless nights left me exhausted and irritable, hindering my development and making it harder to focus in the few fleeting moments of relative calm. The exhaustion compounded the already-present anxieties, creating a vicious cycle of deprivation.

There was a pervasive sense of chaos. The constant change, the instability of our housing situation, and my mother's unpredictable behavior left me with a profound feeling of being adrift, unmoored, and constantly battling a sense of disorientation.

It was as if I were constantly standing on shifting sand, never quite able to find my footing. There was no routine, no sense of order, no predictable rhythm to guide my days. This lack of structure left me feeling lost and vulnerable, constantly anticipating the next unpredictable event.

The world of adults was far too close, far too accessible. I witnessed things a child should have never seen or heard. The conversations I couldn't understand but instinctively knew were alarming. The casualness with which people came and went to the transient nature of my mother's relationships created a disturbing blur of faces and voices, leaving me feeling perpetually on edge.

The blurring of lines between casual acquaintances and more intimate relationships fostered a sense of confusion and unease. The adults in my life, preoccupied with their own struggles and dramas, often overlooked or underestimated my emotional vulnerability. My attempts to make sense of the chaos often resulted in more confusion and a burgeoning sense of shame. This constant exposure to adult anxieties and behaviors created a strange intimacy with the darker aspects of life.

I understood the weight of financial hardship at a far too young age, the desperation of people searching for an escape from poverty or the sting of rejection, all of which played out against the backdrop of my own developing understanding. I learned to read the subtle cues that adults would overlook, anticipating arguments, bracing myself for the inevitable fallout, and becoming adept at avoiding potential conflicts.

The pervasive feeling of being unwanted, unloved, and uncared for shaped my very sense of self. I internalised the message that I was somehow flawed, unworthy of attention, or simply insignificant. This internalised message fueled a deep-seated feeling of shame and self-doubt, a toxic combination that would haunt me for years. The lack of positive reinforcement and the absence of unconditional love created a deep-seated sense of inadequacy. I struggled to develop a healthy self-image, constantly measuring myself against an unattainable ideal. This led to a painful cycle of self-criticism and a pervasive feeling of being inadequate.

The lack of affirmation only further cemented the feeling of worthlessness. Understanding the complexities of this early neglect is vital to understanding the traumas that followed. It wasn't a single, defining moment but the cumulative effect of a myriad of small, insidious events, each chipping away at my sense of security, shaping my understanding of myself, and creating a fertile ground for future exploitation.

The insidious nature of emotional neglect, in stark contrast to the immediate impact of physical abuse, makes it even more difficult to identify and address. It is the absence of something essential, the quiet withholding of care, that becomes the silent assailant, slowly shaping a child's sense of self and their capacity to navigate the world.

The impact of this neglect continues to resonate to this day; its legacy is interwoven into the fabric of my being, shaping my perception of relationships, my trust in others, and my sense of self-worth. Recognising this, acknowledging the subtle but profound ways that early neglect impacted my life, is the first step towards healing and moving forward.

A Shattered Innocence

The memory is still vivid, sharply etched in my mind, despite attempts of my young mind to bury it. The house felt different that day; the usual chaos seemed somehow muted, replaced by an unnerving stillness. My mother was out, and she sent us to the pool for the day that had become a constant in my life. Before leaving home, I remember a smell–a cloying sweetness, something floral and sickly, clinging to the air like a shroud. It's a scent that still triggers a visceral reaction in me, a wave of nausea and dread that washes over me unexpectedly years later.

A family acquaintance, someone my mother had introduced as a "friend" years prior, showed up at the pool, but we called him 'Uncle Larry.' It wasn't until many years after the incident that I discovered he was a known predator and had been in prison for well over a decade. He wasn't frightening in the way of a monster or had a menacing presence. He was… an ordinary, married man with a wife and young child. This ordinariness is perhaps what made it so profoundly unsettling and so utterly insidious. He seemed comfortable, almost paternal in his manner, a stark contrast to the general atmosphere of neglect and instability that defined my life. He was a father figure in a way, as he was always there. This false sense of comfort, this deceptive normalcy, created a guaranteed vulnerability that allowed him to breach my defenses with terrifying ease.

He coaxed me with promises of sweets, games, attention and money–things that were desperately lacking in my own life. There was no violence, no shouting, no overt threat. Instead, there was a subtle manipulation, a quiet seduction that preyed on my loneliness and my yearning for connection.

The details themselves remain vivid but a little fragmented in the timeline as I had known him for years, memories of me often sitting on his lap, his hand on my lower back, bottom or upper thigh, taking me for a drive into the bushland behind the Cluden Racetrack where we would be in scrubland in grass much taller than any of us it had a haunting deeply eerie feel where I would then watch him dig child sized holes in the dirt and then throw in thick black plastic bags and bury them.

My mind thought, *Oh, is that a body or body parts,* as I loved horror movies, something we would also watch at Uncle Larry's, so I asked and he looked at me and didn't say anything. He just remained silent. Once he was finished, he walked towards me with the shovel still in his hands and a strange look in his eyes. It actually scared me deeply to the point I started walking backwards into the grass and I could feel my heart beating faster and things started to go in slow motion.

I stopped but also felt like I was ready to run, I said in my sweetest little boy voice with my eyes like big puppy eyes, "Uncle Larry, we should go home now, you know mum will be looking for me... Come on, let's go home, Uncle Larry."

He stopped and there was just silence. I started walking sideways towards his Toyota Landcruiser, not taking my eyes off him and then it was like a switch had flicked in his eyes, and his face relaxed. He said, "Ok, let's get you home." This was the last time I saw Uncle Larry until the swimming pool incident a few years later.

I would watch Uncle Larry in the shower and take a shower with him at his home while his wife and son were out, or he would touch me in the pool, rubbing himself against me feeling his erect penis through his swim shorts, which I deliberately repressed in my mind over the years. But the feeling... the feeling remains etched into the deepest recesses of my being. A sense of profound violation, of utter helplessness, of being utterly betrayed by someone who should have cared for me and not touched me in that way.

It wasn't a physical pain that dominated; it was the crushing weight of shame, the overwhelming sense of being soiled, tainted, as he was our uncle. He was family, wasn't he? Well, that's what I had grown up to believe otherwise, why call him Uncle? I didn't understand what had happened, not completely. The words were confusing, the actions alien and terrifying. But I understood, on a primal level, that something deeply wrong had occurred. A part of me, a fragile, innocent part, had been stolen, leaving behind a hollow ache that never truly disappeared.

The immediate aftermath is a blur of confused emotions. There was no one to talk to, no one to confide in. My mother's behavior and emotional unavailability rendered her incapable of providing comfort and support. I was scared to tell anyone and she had also just started another relationship with a man named Michael, who would later become my stepfather.

The absence of a stable, nurturing adult figure left me isolated, adrift in a sea of confusion and fear. I tried to make sense of it, to rationalise the event in my child's mind. I told myself it was my fault, that I had somehow invited it, that I deserved it. This self-blame, this internalisation of guilt, became a familiar pattern throughout my childhood and beyond, a poisonous narrative that I would struggle to dismantle for many years to come.

The world felt different after that, subtly altered. The colors seemed less vibrant, the sounds less sharp. Even the simple act of playing, once a source of innocent joy, was tainted with a pervasive sense of unease. My trust, already fragile, shattered completely. The foundations of my sense of self, still precarious from years of neglect, crumbled further. The world, once a place of potential wonder and excitement, became a menacing landscape fraught with danger and uncertainty.

The silence surrounding the event was deafening. There were no conversations, no explanations, no apologies. The memory remained locked away, buried deep within the recesses of my mind, a dark secret that I guarded fiercely. The unspoken truth hung heavy in the air, a palpable weight that cast a long shadow over my childhood. This silence, this lack of acknowledgement became another layer of trauma, compounding the initial violation. It was a silent betrayal, a second wound inflicted by the absence of support and understanding.

The shame was immense, an unbearable burden that I carried alone. I felt dirty, broken, unworthy. I feared that if anyone knew, they would reject me, abandon me, further compounding the isolation and abandonment I already experienced. This fear became ingrained. It wasn't merely the fear of being judged or ostracised; it was the deeply rooted fear of being unloved, unwanted, unworthy of care. This fear shaped my relationships, my perceptions, and my actions throughout my life. It was a constant undercurrent, a quiet voice whispering doubts and insecurities into my ear.

Over the years, there were other incidents, other assaults, each one chipping away at the already fractured remnants of my innocence. But the first assault, the initial violation, remains the most significant. It was the catalyst, the event that irrevocably altered the trajectory of my life. It was a crack in the fragile foundation of my being, a crack that would widen and deepen with each subsequent trauma.

The impact of that first assault wasn't confined to the immediate aftermath; it had a far-reaching and long-lasting effect. It affected my relationships, shaping my ability to trust and form intimate connections.

It left me vulnerable to exploitation, attracting those who could sense my underlying insecurity and vulnerability. It fueled the self-destructive behaviors that characterised a significant part of my adolescence and early adulthood.

Understanding the long-term effects of this early trauma is crucial to understanding my journey toward healing. It wasn't a singular event; it was a turning point, a demarcation line between a childhood already marred by instability and a life defined by the struggle to overcome its devastating consequences. The psychological scars remained long after the physical wounds healed, festering beneath the surface affecting my self-perception, my interactions, and my overall well-being.

I spent years trying to erase the memories, to bury them deep within the recesses of my subconscious. But the memories, though fragmented and distorted, stubbornly persisted. They often resurfaced in unexpected moments, triggered by scents, sounds, seeing someone in a crowd or even fleeting emotions. The repressed memories manifested in nightmares, anxieties, anger, and a pervasive sense of unease. The emotional wounds, though invisible, were deeply ingrained, affecting my ability to form healthy relationships, to trust, and to experience genuine joy.

The journey to healing was long and arduous. It involved confronting the pain, acknowledging the trauma, and gradually rebuilding my sense of self. This process was not easy; it involved confronting the deepest fears, challenging the self-destructive patterns that I had developed, and learning to trust again. The road to recovery was paved with setbacks and relapses. It required courage, resilience, and a relentless commitment to self-discovery.

The silence surrounding the event was, in itself, a form of trauma. The lack of acknowledgment, the absence of support, and the failure of adults in my life to protect me—all contributed to the enduring pain and the profound sense of isolation. This absence of validation fueled feelings of shame and self-blame, reinforcing the damaging narratives I had constructed to cope with the overwhelming trauma. The silence allowed the trauma to fester, to grow into a malignant entity that shaped my life in profound ways. Breaking that silence, finding a voice, and sharing my story became integral to my healing process.

The first assault wasn't just a physical violation; it was a shattering of innocence, a theft of self. It was a profound betrayal of trust, a violation of my most basic human right to safety and security. The impact of that event rippled through my life, shaping my perceptions, my relationships, and my sense of self-worth. It is a story of enduring pain and struggle but also of resilience, healing, and the unwavering power of the human spirit to overcome even the most unimaginable adversity.

Understanding the impact of that first assault is crucial to understanding the complexity of my journey towards healing and self-discovery. It is a journey that continues to this day, a testament to the enduring strength and resilience of the human spirit in the face of unimaginable trauma.

This is the beginning of my story—a story of broken innocence and the enduring search for healing.

Patterns of Abuse and Exploitation

The insidious nature of the abuse wasn't a single, catastrophic event; it was a creeping vine, its tendrils weaving themselves into the fabric of my young life. It wasn't just about the physical acts; it was about the subtle manipulations, the carefully constructed power imbalances, and the systematic erosion of my sense of self.

Looking back, I can see the patterns, the recurring themes that characterised the abuse I endured. There was a consistent pattern of grooming, a slow, deliberate process designed to lower my defenses and make me more susceptible to exploitation.

One of the most chilling aspects of this grooming was the insidious blurring of boundaries. Adults who should have been protecting me instead cultivated a sense of intimacy that was deeply inappropriate. They would shower me with attention, gifts, and seemingly harmless affection, creating a sense of specialness and trust that made me vulnerable to their predatory advances. This carefully constructed intimacy was a tool, a means of gaining my confidence and silencing my inner alarm bells. The affection was a mask, concealing the true nature of their intentions. The manipulation was often subtle, a whisper rather than a shout. They would use my naivete and inexperience against me, twisting words and actions to make me believe that the abuse was somehow my fault, my responsibility. The guilt and shame they instilled were powerful weapons, silencing me and preventing me from seeking help. They would subtly manipulate situations, isolating me from the adults who might have intervened, creating a world where their actions appeared normal, even acceptable.

It's a terrifying realisation recognising how easily a child can be manipulated and controlled. The power imbalance was stark and unrelenting. As a child, I was entirely at the mercy of adults. I lacked the emotional maturity, the physical strength, and the social awareness to resist their advances. My vulnerability was their leverage, a tool they exploited with chilling efficiency.

The abuse wasn't a spontaneous act of aggression; it was a calculated violation, a deliberate exploitation of my innocence and defenselessness. The emotional and psychological consequences were profound and long-lasting. The feelings of powerlessness, betrayal, and shame were deeply embedded in my psyche, shaping my perception of myself and my relationships with others. The constant anxiety, the fear of discovery, and the profound sense of isolation created a dark cloud that hung over my childhood. The innocence that should have been a birthright was stolen from me, leaving a gaping wound that would take years to heal.

The recurring nature of the abuse exacerbated its impact. Each incident reinforced the feelings of powerlessness and vulnerability, creating a vicious cycle of fear and self-doubt. The repetition of these acts solidified the belief that this was somehow normal that I deserved this treatment. The insidious normalisation of abuse is a devastating consequence, slowly chipping away at a child's sense of self-worth and dignity.

This normalisation extended beyond the individual acts of abuse. It permeated my entire world, impacting my perception of relationships, intimacy, and even my own body. The constant threat of abuse fostered a deep-seated distrust of adults, making it difficult to form healthy attachments and seek support when I needed it most. The subtle yet pervasive effects of this constant threat manifested in many ways, creating a deep-seated sense of unease and a constant hyper-vigilance that followed me into adulthood.

The trauma was further complicated by the fact that many of the perpetrators were people I knew and trusted. This betrayal of trust added another layer of complexity to the abuse, shattering my sense of safety and security. The feelings of violation were compounded by the profound sense of betrayal, eroding my ability to trust anyone, even those who genuinely cared about me. The violation wasn't just physical; it was a violation of the most fundamental human need: the need for safety and security.

The silence surrounding the abuse was another insidious element. I was too young to fully comprehend what was happening, and even if I had, the fear of repercussions prevented me from speaking out. The adults in my life, those who should have protected me, either didn't notice, didn't believe me, or simply chose to ignore what was happening.

The weight of this silence, the burden of carrying this secret alone, added to the trauma, leaving me feeling isolated and utterly alone in my suffering. The profound impact of this enforced silence is something that continues to resonate with me today.

The experiences I endured weren't just isolated incidents; they were interconnected, forming a pattern of abuse that had a devastating impact on my development. The patterns were subtle yet powerful, eroding my sense of self, distorting my perception of relationships, and leaving me with a profound sense of shame and guilt. This insidious pattern only deepened the trauma, leaving an indelible mark on my psyche.

The systematic nature of the abuse, the way it repeated and escalated over time, solidified the feelings of powerlessness and hopelessness. Each incident left a scar, deepening the wound and making it harder to heal. It wasn't just a matter of surviving the individual incidents; it was a matter of surviving the ongoing pattern of abuse. The cumulative effect of these experiences was profound and far-reaching.

Recognising these patterns is crucial for understanding the long-term effects of childhood trauma. It's not enough to simply label the abuse; we need to understand the mechanisms of manipulation, the dynamics of power, and the subtle ways in which perpetrators gain control and maintain their dominance. Understanding these mechanisms is not only crucial for the healing process but also for preventing future abuse.

The emotional fallout from this continued abuse was staggering. The constant fear, the pervasive sense of shame, and the profound feelings of isolation contributed to a sense of detachment, a feeling of being disconnected from myself and the world around me. I developed coping mechanisms to manage the pain, but these mechanisms often compounded the problem, leading to further self-destruction and reinforcing the cycle of abuse.

These experiences left me struggling to form healthy relationships, haunted by a deep-seated fear of intimacy and a pervasive sense of distrust. The ability to trust others was shattered, leaving me unable to form healthy attachments and creating a profound sense of loneliness. It was a challenging path to recovery, learning to trust again, to form healthy bonds, and to rebuild my sense of self.

The road to healing was long and arduous, fraught with setbacks and challenges. But through therapy, self-reflection, and the unwavering support of others, I began to understand the impact of the abuse and to find ways to cope with the pain. This journey, though difficult, was ultimately one of resilience, empowerment, and the reclamation of my life. It was a testament to the incredible strength of the human spirit, the ability to overcome adversity and find hope even in the darkest of times. And this is the story I share, hoping that it will provide comfort, understanding, and hope to others who have been through similar experiences.

The Role of Family and Acquaintances

The insidiousness of the abuse wasn't confined to the acts themselves. It was woven into the very fabric of my relationships, a tapestry of betrayal stitched with silence and complicity. My family, the people who were supposed to protect me, were often the ones who failed me most profoundly. My mother, struggling with her own demons, was frequently absent, emotionally unavailable, and often oblivious to the dangers surrounding me. Her chaotic lifestyle–marked by unstable relationships and a transient existence–exposed me to environments where I was vulnerable and easily exploited. She wasn't malicious, not intentionally, but her inability to provide a safe and stable environment created a void that predators readily filled.

One specific incident stands out, etched in my memory with a clarity that time cannot erase. I was around 7 years old, and we were living in a small, house in Hermit Park. Robert, a friend of my mother's, frequently visited. He was charming in a way that felt both unsettling and alluring to a child desperate for attention. He would bring small gifts, candy, and sometimes toys, showering me with affection that felt distinctly inappropriate. His touch lingered too long; his words carried a subtle undercurrent of something sinister. The grooming was subtle; the shift from friendly gestures to something predatory was gradual, so gradual that I barely registered it until it was too late. He was looking after me for the night, and my sister was asleep. He said do you want to stay up late and play a game, but you can't tell anyone, or you will get in trouble for staying up late. We played Doctors. I was the patient. He took my faded pyjamas off and laid me down in the front room so he could hear anyone coming up the driveway.

Robert began to touch me then it started ticking. I laughed, he laughed and said it's fun, isn't it I just laid there in silence. He touched my whole body, looking at me, staring into my eyes, blowing raspberries on my tummy and getting lower each time, touching my little willy, kissing me all over my small naked body. He turned me over and was looking at my bottom, tickling my bum and spreading my bum cheeks, looking at me.

Looking back, I understand now that my perception was skewed, my understanding of boundaries distorted by my desperate need for love and acceptance. His actions were predatory, exploiting my vulnerability and my naive understanding of the adult world.

The second event was when I was 10 years old, I was staying with my Grandmother in her housing commission unit at Morell Court in Belgian Gardens. My aunt and uncle also lived in the same housing commission complex. Tony, a long-term family friend who lived with his mother on the second floor of the third block of apartments at the back, was a nice, funny young man. He had a job in the mines and his mother was a church-going woman who often talked with me and made me a sandwich. When Tony was away at work, she would let me sit in his room and watch movies while he was away.

One afternoon Tony was home and I was so happy to see him. I asked if I could watch a movie he said yes, I have a new one called Dune. Tony advised his mother he was going to watch a movie and would close the door so as not to bother her. I sat on his single bed all excited, the room was small and hot. He opened the window a little and we both lay on the bed and watched the movie, his big, strong arm around my chest as we laid back. After a while, it was getting hotter, so Tony said he wanted to take his shirt off and I should do the same, so I did.

I laid back down against his hairy, sweaty chest. It was sticky and tickled me a little. He laughed and said, it's ok. You will be hairy one day. After a little more time had passed, he said he was still hot and was going to take all his clothes off and said it was ok. The door is locked. Mum won't know. He proceeded to get naked. I was surprised he was like a muscular, hairy bear. I remember saying you look like a teddy bear he laughed and said your turn to take your shorts off so I did and we laid back on the bed and continued to watch the movie. His arm was over my stomach and I remember his penis pushed against my upper thigh. Tony slowly stroked my hip. It was calming in a way. He said he was feeling love and I felt and saw his penis pulse against my thigh. I asked what's that he said he loved me and wanted to be my best friend. He asked if I would be his best friend, and I said yes.

Tony asked if he could touch me. I didn't realise what this really meant but I soon worked out he wanted me to touch him in return. I remember touching his hairy chest and nipples. They were hard and not soft like mine. He touched me gently all over my body, and by this time, he had an erection and to my eyes, it was not small. He convinced me to touch his penis, moving it back and forth in my small hand.

I had never done this before I didn't know what I was doing. Tony assured me it was ok and it is what boys do, he said he was going to put his penis in my mouth, and I had to be quiet or his mum would hear us and I would get in trouble. He proceeded to put his thick, circumcised penis into my mouth and moved it in and out while he was playing with his testicles and the shaft of his penis. After a short time, he pushed it deeper and harder into my mouth. I remember tasting sweat and the coarse, dark brown, thick, curly pubic hair. He grabbed my head and pushed again, my eyes bulging with shock, surprise and fear. I wanted it to stop tears running from my eyes. He held me and kept going. I was trying to push him away, but I had no chance of doing that.

Tony ejaculated; it went down my throat, in my mouth and on my chin. He said it's ok. I love you. This is our secret. I was in shock; it felt like everything was in slow motion. I got dressed and ran out of the unit, not even saying goodbye to his mother and I went and hid for what felt like hours in the tall grass on the hill behind the complex. I wiped the semen from my face and spat out what I could taste. I didn't know what happened. I was lost in my own head and I couldn't tell anyone. My grandmother called me as it was getting dark and I went inside and had a bath and I never spoke of this to anyone for years.

The third incident was when I was 12 and it was with another family friend that we called Uncle Larry. I mentioned a little of this earlier. This was a grooming that went on for years: a touch here, a hand there, sitting on his lap, being alone with him on so many occasions, him giving me treats, toys money. But Uncle Larry was also a known predator and had already served substantial time in prison for a murder in the 1960s, but I didn't know that at the time. It was something my mother told me a few years later when I was older, she said we needed to keep away from him at all costs as he was a very dangerous man. Prior to this knowledge, Uncle Larry was like the others: unassuming, gentle and loving, A family man with a young child and wife, but he used to spend a lot of time with us kids, showing up randomly, seeing him outside our school or just showing up in the park I'd be excited and yell Uncle Larry and give him a hug, he said I've come to take you home but let's go for ice-cream or a drive first you mum said to pick you up. Only to find out later my mother never asked him to pick us up it was all made up.

I would jump excitedly into his Toyota Landcruiser. It was such a big truck to me, and I loved it. I would sit right up against Uncle Larry and sometimes he would let me use the gear stick with his hand on mine. Well, this was another wolf in sheep's clothing. He would woo us with adventures, lollies, toys and money.

One hot summer afternoon at the pool, I saw Uncle Larry walking along the pool fence looking in, and he called out. I got excited and ran over and said hello. We talked for a bit, then he said he would come in and play with us. Uncle Larry came into the pool and started playing with us kids. After a while, he got physical with a touch that lasted longer than it should, holding me against himself, playing around in the pool as kids do, moving around in the water. Larry was fixated on being close to me, very close; we were constantly in physical contact in the water. Then it happened. I could feel his penis through his shorts against me, then it would stop as he would change positions or pull me against him. Hence, a different part of my body was against him again. I could feel his erect penis against me and feel it through his shorts. This went on for a few minutes. He looked at me and smiled and then it was time to leave.

We got out of the pool and went for showers. We were both naked and he was touching himself and getting excited with the soap and offered to soap up my back. I said, ok, Uncle Larry. He came over and soaped me up and then ended up soaping up my whole body using the excuse he had to get me clean because of my delicate skin and the chlorine in the pool. He asked me to wash his back, so I did and eventually, we left the pool and instead of taking me home, he took me to his place as his wife and son were not home. I had been to their house many times to play with their son and watch movies and sleep over, so I didn't think anything of it.

After a few minutes, I heard the shower running and he came out naked and said he was going to have another shower, and he could still smell chlorine. I thought, *Ok.* I was happy watching The Muppet Show on video as, at the time, it was my favourite. He came out again and said you need to have another shower because of the chlorine, and as he was an adult, I looked up to my Uncle and did what he asked.

I went into the shower, it was a small shower over bath and got naked. He hopped in the shower with me, washed me down and soaped up his body. He was tall and fit and had what appeared to be a large circumcised penis. He was erect in moments and it was right in my line of sight. Larry started playing with it in the shower. I felt uncomfortable, but I just stood there and watched him. I was kind of fascinated at how big it was, as mine was only small, but then again, I was only a child.

I was not excited by this and was getting cold standing at the other end of the shower, but it wasn't long before he wanted to touch me. He did, but it was more around soaping me up and washing me. He ejaculated into the floor of the bath and down the drain it went. He then rinsed off, and we got dressed. Then he took me home and gave me $50, and said don't tell anyone about today and here is some money for you and your mum to get pizza for dinner. Now, that excited me. I got home and Mum was surprised I had seen Uncle Larry and that he gave us some money, but he was always doing things like that and helping out where he could.

The fourth time I was assaulted was brutal. I was 14 years old and assaulted by an Indigenous man (now deceased). Let's call him Prior and his friend Jarred.

Prior was a man from a well-known Indigenous family that had regular police trouble. Both of these men lived in a suburb called Rasmussen on Riverway Drive. They lived down from the Gumvale shops past the youth group house that was next to the Pastor's house. I know this as it was my local area.

I was on my way to the church youth group. I was in my own little world, humming gospel tunes in my head and looking forward to seeing my friends and my new girlfriend.

On the way there, I was stopped by two men, one an Indigenous man named Prior and the other a Caucasian boy with red hair named Jarred. I had recognised Jarred as I had seen him before as he lived next to the pastor's house and the church youth group house I was part of, but I did not know Prior or Jarred personally; I only knew of them.

Prior started being aggressive and was threatening me and intimidating me. Jarred was egging him on and also being threatening; I couldn't get away from them. Every time I tried, they would stop me with threats and violence. I was hit several times and dragged off to some bushes where the further assault took place while his friend Jarred stood there and watched everything.

I was crying and saying, "No, no, don't do this."

My clothes were torn off, my necklace and cross were ripped from my neck, and he hit me again. I fell to the ground. I remember everything being like I was dizzy. My ears were ringing, things went into slow motion, and I could taste the dirt in my mouth.

I thought this couldn't be real. It couldn't be happening. I just wished someone would find us and save me. I was pulled up from the ground and then he pushed me back down. I was crying and all I kept saying through the whole ordeal was no, don't do this, stop, stop, please stop, please don't hit me, but he just hit me again and again.

He pulled down his pants and pulled out his penis. He had an erection and then played with it a little and moved towards me and pushed it into my face and said, "Suck it."

I turned my head away and said, "No."

He started hitting me again and said aggressively "put it in your mouth and suck it". Jarred was watching from about 2m away. I think he was on the lookout. I did what Prior asked. I turned my head and he pushed his large erect penis into my mouth. He said look at me. He was violent, nasty and horrible to me. He then spat in my face. I turned my head away and spat out his penis. He pulled me back and screamed suck it and pushed it back into my mouth. He was getting rougher and rougher then he grabbed my hair and pushed deeper and deeper he raped my face and throat. I was crying, there were tears and snot running down my face and I was choking and gagging on his big, circumcised black penis.

I didn't like what was happening in any way. I was not excited in any way; I was terrified. How could this be happening? This was a living hell. I wish I was dead. How could God let this happen to me? After a few minutes, he stopped raping my face and pushed me onto the ground and said bend over. I was on my hands and knees he walked around me, saying stop crying, shut up, be quiet, I watched him spit on his hand and wipe it on his penis and then he approached me again, but this time from behind. He then pushed his erect penis into my bottom. It didn't go in. He tried again and spat on his penis and kept pushing and pushing, moving back and forth. He pushed it into my bottom. Oh, the pain was excruciating. It was hurting even when he pulled it out, then he would push it back in, all the way in. It was getting faster and faster. He was very forceful and rough. I was crying and tried to scream out, but he had covered my mouth with his hand and he continued doing so for what felt like an eternity. He hurt me in a way I had never known, as I was a virgin and had never had sex myself. I had only been the victim of abuse. Prior ejaculated and then pushed me back to the ground and kicked me. He pulled up his pants and said to Jarred your turn, Jarred declined. I could not understand why he watched this happen to me all that time and did nothing to help me. He was just as evil as Prior and enjoyed watching what was happening.

I was then told if I told anyone, they would find me and kill me and they left laughing. I was left lying in the dirt, in the bushes half, clothed, crying and in pain. I slowly pulled myself together and slowly walked towards home, feeling numb and lost. I went to a friend's place as I couldn't go home like this, I told my friend Adrian and his brother Mark. They were horrified at what I had told them, and they immediately took me to another friend's place, another friend of my mother's, Uncle Tony and Aunt Sally, but they weren't really my relatives. They called the police and while we were waiting for them to arrive, I cleaned myself up in the bathroom. During that, I heard Uncle Tony say Joey must have deserved it because he is very feminine and has a lesbian mother. It cut me deeply to hear them say that as they had known me and my mum for as long as I could remember, and they only lived about 7 houses away from my mum.

The police arrived and took a statement from me and then took me to the hospital for a checkup and tests in a secure section of the hospital. The hospital was a void of people in the area I was in and the halls were empty, the police stayed with me at all times, as it was now the early hours of the morning. The doctor checked me over and was very nice even though the tests were very invasive, the police took all my clothes as evidence and bagged and tagged it. I was cold and violated, feeling internally numb. I was there for hours and watched the sun come up through the windows. I was left sitting there in a hospital gown and they eventually said I could go home and the police then took me back to the police station and then took me home.

When I got home, I explained what happened to Margaret, a friend I was living with. She said I needed to go next door to my mum's place and talk to my mum and my stepfather about it. I didn't go into great detail. All I said was I was sexually assaulted and had been at the hospital all night. My stepfather was so angry with what had happened that he punched a hole in the wall and my mum cried and gave me a hug. A few days later, my stepfather made me walk to the Prior's house and call them out to talk to them; however, being Indigenous, he had a large number of his family come out. There were 7 people there and they started to move around the yard so they were on both sides of us. It was very confronting Prior was there and he was just staring at me. I wanted to run away; I was getting scared again. My stepfather, an ex-military man, told me to leave right away and go straight home as fast as I could, so I left. My dad stayed and came home a little later. I am not sure if he said anything or if anything happened. I didn't want to know and have never asked him what happened.

This was a horrific situation. I had never felt like this, and it had gone around the whole neighbourhood like wildfire. My family didn't like it and were very concerned for me, I had withdrawn internally. I wanted to kill myself and tried to hang myself in a tree behind the church youth group but was stopped by friends. The weight of this was too much for me. I felt like all my friends had disowned me. I felt like it was all my fault for not fighting back more.

My aunty was called and it was decided I would go away to another town for a few months until things settled down and I felt better. I agreed to go away with her and my cousin. I thought we were meant to go to Cairns, but she had moved to another town called Gayndah. Before we left town, we stopped at the Kirwan Police Station to let them know what was happening. My aunty had told me to drop the assault and rape charges. I didn't want to drop them, but she forced me to drop the charges. The police officer was a lovely lady and she urged me not to do that as this person was well known to them. They had also questioned the friend, and they had good evidence, but my aunt kept saying it would be an embarrassment on the family name and we just needed it to go away and if I went through with the charges then it would be with me forever. So that was why I was forced to withdraw it.

After a few months in Gaynda, a very small country town in Queensland, I came back home to my mum and dad. It wasn't long before the family violence started again, the screaming, slamming doors, smashed dishes, and bruises, but this time, I stood up to him and stood between him and my mum, and that was it. I was thrown out of my home at 15 and living on the street. He wanted me gone. My mum said to my dad, "No, it was his home before it was yours. He stayed, but it was not any environment for a child going through what I was going through." I packed a bag, took my pillow and my snoopy teddy bear, I left school and had to fend for myself. I started sleeping outside abandoned houses and, behind shop dumpsters and in gardens.

The silence surrounding these events was deafening. There was a tacit understanding, a collective unwillingness to acknowledge what was happening. My mother, family and friends, preoccupied with their own struggles, seemingly missed or chose to ignore the warning signs. Perhaps they were afraid to confront reality, afraid of the implications, afraid of what it might mean about their own judgment and their ability to protect me. Whatever their reasons, the silence was a form of complicity, a failure to protect and support a child and that continues to haunt me to this day. All I thought was, what about me? What about how I feel? They were meant to love me.

This pattern repeated itself with other adults in my life. They were either part of the LGBTQIA+ family or acquaintances, friends fathers and even neighbours who crossed the line, their actions ranging from inappropriate touching to outright abuse. These encounters were often interspersed with periods of relative calm, lulls that only served to intensify the trauma when the abuse inevitably resurfaced. The unpredictability and the inconsistency made it even harder to process what was happening to understand that these actions weren't my fault.

The feeling of betrayal was overwhelming; the people I trusted, the people who were supposed to love, support and protect me, were actively harming me. The lack of intervention from the adults in my life speaks volumes about the broader societal issues that enable child abuse. There was a pervasive culture of silence, an unwillingness to acknowledge the problem, to intervene, or even to believe a child's account of abuse. This silence served as a protective shield for the abusers, allowing them to continue their predatory behaviour unchecked. The adults, either through ignorance, denial, or a conscious choice to turn a blind eye, perpetuated a cycle of abuse that left me feeling isolated, powerless, and deeply alone.

The shame and guilt that followed these encounters were intense and pervasive. I internalised the message that I was somehow responsible for what happened, that I had done something to provoke these actions. The self-blame was a constant companion, a heavy weight that I carried for years. It warped my perception of myself, fostering a deep-seated sense of worthlessness and unlovability. I struggled with feelings of intense anger and confusion, not knowing who to trust or where to turn for help. The ongoing instability in my home life exacerbated this internal conflict.

Beyond the immediate perpetrators, there were also instances where adults failed to intervene when they had the opportunity. There were times when I confided in family, friends, and even neighbours only to be met with disbelief, dismissal, or a lack of understanding, saying I brought it on myself and not to do anything as it would bring shame to the family. The lack of appropriate response left me feeling more alone and isolated than ever. These moments of missed opportunity to protect me, to intervene and prevent further harm, and the lack of any professional help amplified the feeling of abandonment and deepened the sense of betrayal.

The cumulative effect of these betrayals was devastating, it eroded my sense of trust, making it incredibly difficult to form healthy relationships. The fear of being hurt again and the constant anxiety that someone would violate my boundaries became a defining characteristic of my life for many years. It impacted my ability to trust anyone, leaving me feeling isolated and emotionally disconnected.

The emotional fallout extended far beyond the physical abuse. I developed deep-seated anxiety, depression, and likely undiagnosed post-traumatic stress disorder (PTSD). How does a child of 15 deal with all of this? Well they can't, certainly not alone.

These conditions manifested in various ways, including nightmares, flashbacks, difficulty sleeping, and emotional dysregulation. I struggled to maintain healthy relationships, experiencing significant challenges with intimacy and trust. I avoided forming close bonds for fear of repeating my past experiences. The fear of vulnerability was so overwhelming that I built emotional walls around myself, creating a protective shield that prevented intimacy.

My journey to recovery has been long and arduous, filled with setbacks and periods of intense emotional pain. However, therapy, self-reflection, and the unwavering support of those who eventually understood and believed me have been instrumental in my healing process. Understanding the systemic nature of the abuse, recognising that it wasn't my fault, and accepting the role played by the adults in my life–their inaction as much as their active participation has been a crucial step in my journey to reclaim my life.

The road to recovery isn't linear; it's a winding path, full of ups and downs, but I am committed to moving forward, living a life free from the shadow of my past. The wounds may remain and always will, but they no longer define me.

I share my story not for sympathy, but for understanding and to help others who have endured similar experiences to find hope and begin their own journeys of healing and resilience. The power of silence enabled the abuse; breaking that silence sharing my story, is a powerful act of reclaiming my life.

Survival through Sex: A Cycle of Abuse

The instability of my childhood wasn't just about the physical moves; it was the constant shifting of my sense of safety and belonging. One minute, I was in a relatively stable (though impoverished) environment; then everything would unravel. My mother's relationships were volatile, often ending abruptly, leaving us scrambling to find new housing, new schools, and new–often precarious–sources of income. This constant upheaval left me feeling adrift, profoundly insecure, and hyper-vigilant. It also made me incredibly vulnerable.

In this environment, survival became a daily, almost primal, instinct. Food was often scarce, and the simple act of securing a meal could be a struggle. Clean clothes, a warm bed, even a sense of basic comfort –these were luxuries I rarely enjoyed. The adults in my life, even those who claimed to care, were often consumed by their own problems. My needs were secondary, an afterthought in their chaotic lives.

The first time I was chorused to engage in sexual activity, and I allowed it to happen, was to get something I needed–food, shelter, a place to sleep–it was a blur of confusion and shear desperation.

I was young, going through puberty, and still grappling with the complexities of my body and its burgeoning sexuality. The act itself was more of a transaction, a desperate exchange for necessities. It wasn't about pleasure or even desire; it was pure survival. It was about silencing the gnawing hunger, escaping the cold, or finding a temporary reprieve from the constant fear that characterised my life.

Shame immediately followed. The feeling wasn't so much about the act itself–though there was undoubtedly shame associated with that–but the deep-seated sense of violation and degradation. It felt like a profound betrayal of my own innocence, a shattering of my already fragile sense of self.

This shame became a heavy cloak I wore, a secret I guarded fiercely, a burden that compounded the trauma I had already endured. The cycle began innocently, or rather, it began without my consent or understanding. I'd been used to being the recipient of unwanted advances, a silent observer in scenarios where boundaries were routinely disregarded. The line between 'ok' and 'not ok' became increasingly blurred in that haze of neglect and abuse. My perception of normalcy had been skewed, and my understanding of healthy relationships was distorted.

The transactional nature of the encounters was striking. It wasn't about affection, connection, or mutual desire. It was a stark and brutal exchange of sex for basic needs. Food for Sex. Shelter for Sex. Safety for Sex. These were the terms of my survival, and I was a participant in a system where my worth was reduced to my body and its capacity for sexual gratification.

At first, I thought of myself as being somehow complicit; I believed that if I wasn't so needy, so desperate, this wouldn't have happened. This notion of personal responsibility is a cruel twist of the trauma narrative–a self-blame that keeps victims locked in a perpetual cycle of self-recrimination. The reality, however, is that the blame rests squarely on the shoulders of those who preyed on my vulnerability and exploited my desperate need for basic necessities.

They were the adults–and some were older children who knew better and yet chose to act in ways that deeply harmed me.

The cycle escalated subtly. What started as isolated incidents became more frequent and more calculated. I began to anticipate the pattern: a display of kindness, a moment of empathy, followed by an insidious shift into manipulation and coercion. The promises of food, shelter, or protection were often empty, or worse, they served only as tools to keep me trapped in the cycle of abuse.

The manipulation wasn't always overt. It was woven into the fabric of my interactions, disguised as concern, disguised as friendship. There were smiles and gentle words, creating an illusion of caring and support before the inevitable demands emerged. This subtle manipulation is a hallmark of sexual abuse, a cruel tactic used to disarm and control the victim.

Moreover, the sense of powerlessness was crippling. I was perpetually dependent on others for my basic needs; these dependencies became leverage points for exploitation. I felt trapped, without the resources or support network to escape the abuse. The sense of isolation was overwhelming; I believed that no one would believe me, that no one would care. This belief, unfortunately, proved to be partly true.

The isolation deepened as I became more deeply entangled in the cycle of abuse. I kept the secret buried beneath layers of shame and fear, afraid to speak out for fear of further retribution or rejection. The silence became a prison, compounding the trauma and reinforcing my sense of powerlessness. This silence was a testament to the insidious nature of the abuse, its ability to erode self-worth and confidence to the point of complete incapacitation. The effect on my self-image was profound. My worth became inextricably linked to my sexual availability and my ability to provide sexual gratification to others. This twisted perspective distorted my sense of self, shaping my view of my own body and sexuality in a deeply unhealthy way. I was conditioned to believe that I had no value beyond my physical body.

The emotional consequences were devastating. Trust was shattered. The idea of intimacy and genuine connection became warped and distorted, replaced by a deep-seated fear and mistrust. I struggled to form healthy relationships, constantly anticipating betrayal and exploitation. The ability to develop healthy attachments was compromised; the experience had permanently scarred my capacity for genuine connection and emotional intimacy.

As time went on, the pattern of abuse began to feel normal. It became an ingrained aspect of my reality, a way of life, a tragic but inescapable part of my existence. The normalisation of this abuse is a chilling aspect of the trauma, a cruel twist that strips victims of their agency and reinforces the insidious grip of the abuser.

The impact of this early exposure to transactional sex with doctors, a priest, a university professor, government employees, Military Men RAAF, Navy, Army, a florist and a hairdresser — all these men were seeking this type of exploitation in Townsville and it impacted my self-worth and adult relationships.

It shaped my understanding of love and intimacy, making it exceptionally difficult to form healthy relationships. I found myself seeking out relationships that replicated the power dynamics of my past, unconsciously drawn to intellectuals and individuals who demonstrated similar patterns of manipulative behaviour.

In therapy, years later, I began to untangle the complexities of this period. I came to understand that the transactional sex was not my fault. It was a survival mechanism in an environment characterised by extreme deprivation and a profound lack of safety.

Understanding this did not erase the pain, but it did give me a new perspective on my actions, allowing me to forgive myself for the choices I made in my desperation.

The journey of healing is ongoing and always will be. It's a process of reclaiming my body, my sexuality, and my sense of self. It is a journey marked by self-compassion, self-acceptance and a willingness to confront the complex realities of my past. This understanding, coupled with the unwavering support of my therapist and loved ones, has empowered me to take back my narrative and live a life free from the shadow of my past.

The experience has led me to be able to support others who have experienced similar trauma. I now understand the insidious nature of abuse, its subtle forms of coercion, and the lasting impact it can have on an individual's life. Knowing my own experience makes me better equipped to empathise, offer support, and provide a safe space for those who have survived similar harrowing experiences. The pain remains, but sharing my story is part of my process of healing and empowerment.

It is my way of transforming trauma into a catalyst for growth, resilience, and meaningful change. It's my way of breaking the cycle of silence, of ensuring that no one else has to endure what I have. My story is not just about surviving; it's about thriving despite the unimaginable.

Homelessness and Exploitation on the Streets

The instability that had characterised my early life culminated in homelessness. It wasn't a sudden event but a slow, agonising descent. First, there were the increasingly frequent nights spent sleeping on friends' couches or a floor, a temporary reprieve that always ended. Then came the beach and park benches, offering little protection from the elements, the chilling dampness seeping into my bones, the biting wind a constant reminder of my vulnerability. The city lights, once a source of fascination, now felt like cold, indifferent eyes watching my plight.

The smell of the city became a visceral memory–a pungent mix of exhaust fumes, stale urine, and decaying garbage. These scents were etched into my memory, a constant olfactory reminder of my desperate situation. The sounds, too, were unrelenting: the rumble of traffic, the distant sirens, the shouts and laughter of others. Indigenous people sleeping, drinking and fighting in the streets. Everyone knew you had to avoid the park people, all blending into a cacophony that mirrored the chaos within me. The city, once a place of possibility, was now a threatening landscape, a constant battle for survival.

Hunger became a gnawing, persistent companion. The pangs in my stomach were a relentless reminder of my poverty, a constant, physical manifestation of my deprivation. I scavenged for food, searching through dumpsters behind restaurants and supermarkets, sorting through discarded scraps, hoping to find something edible. The shame was almost unbearable, the humiliation a weight heavier than the gnawing hunger, so I started walking around supermarkets eating bananas, nuts and steggles chicken roll and not paying for them. Even the smallest offering of food, a stale crust of bread, became a precious commodity, a symbol of unexpected kindness in a world that seemed overwhelmingly cruel.

Sleep was a luxury I rarely afforded. The constant fear of attack, of theft, or simply of being moved on by the authorities kept me on edge. Sleep came in short, restless bursts, punctuated by jolts of adrenaline and anxieties. My body ached from the cold, the hard surfaces of the ground or benches, and the lack of proper rest. My clothes were threadbare, offering little protection from the harsh elements.

My naivety about the dangers of the streets was quickly dispelled. I witnessed violence, both subtle and brutal, on a regular basis. Arguments escalated into fights, often involving knives or other weapons. I saw drug deals go down in the shadows, overheard whispered conversations about exploitation, and witnessed the desperation that drove people to make desperate choices. The veneer of civilisation had been stripped away, revealing a brutal underbelly that was both terrifying and strangely fascinating.

The vulnerability of being homeless opened me up to exploitation, a chilling and insidious form of abuse. I was approached by older men, and their intentions were clear and predatory. The offers of food, shelter, or money were subtle forms of coercion, often delivered with a disarming friendliness that masked their underlying intentions. The power dynamic was stark, my desperation making me susceptible to their manipulations. I learned to navigate this treacherous landscape to decipher the subtle cues that could signal danger. I honed my survival instincts, developing a hyper-awareness of my surroundings, always scanning for potential threats. My body became my shield, my eyes my weapons and boy, could I run.

The streets became a school of hard knocks, teaching me harsh lessons about human nature, about survival, and about the devastating consequences of vulnerability. I learned to read people, to anticipate their intentions, and to protect myself as best as I could. But it was a constant, exhausting battle, a relentless struggle against the elements, the hunger, the fear, and the ever-present threat of exploitation.

One particular encounter stands out, not for its uniqueness–as such experiences became horrifyingly commonplace–but for its chilling normality. A man older, with eyes that held a mixture of pity and something darker, offered me a place to sleep for the night. He wasn't overtly threatening, but his demeanour held a subtle undercurrent of menace. The offer seemed like a lifeline, a temporary escape from the harsh realities of the streets. But deep down, I knew it was a dangerous proposition, a gamble with consequences I couldn't fully comprehend.

The room was cramped, dingy, and smelled of stale cigarettes and there were pill bottles on the floor and something else, something indefinably unpleasant. He tried to be friendly, saying he was a meteorologist he offered me food and drink. I was concerned the drink might have been drugged, so I didn't drink it. I poured it into a plant when he wasn't looking and pretended to drink it.

His touch was possessive and firm, his gaze unsettling and he kept wanting to kiss me. I didn't do that as that was too intimate and I couldn't control my feelings when it came to intimacy like that, it was odd, but it is just how I am. I remained alert and on edge, my senses heightened. I felt I was in a fight or flight mode, constantly assessing the situation and looking for the best escape route if anything bad happened that I didn't like, but he had deadlocked the door, so that wasn't an option for escape. His windows were tinted and locked; however, I managed to escape in the early hours of the morning while he was asleep by jumping down from the bedroom balcony, leaving behind a sense of dread that lingered for days.

That night, I learned a valuable lesson about trusting my instincts, even when the consequences of not trusting them seemed far worse than the uncertainty of the streets. It was sometime later, I met someone who knew the meteorologist and they told me he had committed suicide and it was a shock to people, but it supposedly had something to do with an underage boy he had seen and the guilt of it, I automatically felt bad and sad for him and thought I hope it wasn't me, had I led him to his death by running away, was he in a dark place and needed someone was I the catalyst that tipped him over the edge it haunted me for years.

In a cruel irony, sex became a means of survival. It wasn't about pleasure in any way; it was about basic necessities–food, a place to sleep, some clothes or a fleeting moment of perceived safety. The shame was immense, a heavy cloak of guilt that weighed me down. I felt violated, dirty, used and utterly worthless. These encounters weren't consensual; they were acts of desperation born out of vulnerability and the stark realities of homelessness. They were survival transactions, a grim exchange of bodily integrity for the most basic needs.

The physical toll was significant. The lack of proper food, sleep, and hygiene took its toll on my body. I was constantly battling exhaustion, hunger and the lingering psychological scars of repeated trauma and I had become afraid of the dark. My body, once a symbol of youthful energy, became vulnerable, a constant reminder of my experiences. I was 52kg and 175cm tall, so quite underweight.

The emotional scars were even deeper, leaving me with a sense of hopelessness, worthlessness, and profound isolation.

Despite the darkness, however, glimmers of hope persisted. Acts of unexpected kindness–a warm meal from a stranger, a kind word from a passerby, a moment of shared empathy–offered brief respites from the despair. These small acts of compassion, though infrequent, were crucial in sustaining my fragile hope. They were a reminder that humanity wasn't completely extinguished and that some people still possessed the capacity for empathy and kindness in a world that often seemed devoid of both. They were moments that kept the embers of my spirit alive, preventing me from completely succumbing to the darkness.

The experience of homelessness and street exploitation profoundly shaped my understanding of the world and my place within it. It forced me to confront the harsh realities of poverty, inequality, and the vulnerability of those who fall through the cracks of society. The memories are still vivid, and the emotional wounds are still raw, but sharing them is part of my healing journey. It's my way of transforming trauma into a catalyst for change, ensuring that others don't have to endure what I did.

My story is a testament to the resilience of the human spirit, the capacity for hope even in the darkest of times, and the importance of recognising and addressing the vulnerabilities that lead to exploitation and abuse. It is a story about survival, but ultimately, a story about thriving. It is a story about reclaiming my life, my identity, and my voice.

The journey was arduous, but it led me to a place of healing and, ultimately, to a profound understanding of the importance of compassion and support for those who have endured similar experiences. The scars remain, but they serve as a powerful reminder of my strength and resilience, a testament to the enduring power of the human spirit.

The Weight of Silence and Shame

The weight of what happened settled on me like a shroud, suffocating and inescapable. It wasn't just the physical pain, though the memory of rough hands and violated boundaries still sent shivers down my spine years later. It was the crushing weight of silence, a silence so profound it felt as though it had been woven into the very fabric of my being. I carried it like a secret shame, a heavy burden I couldn't share, didn't know how to share, and perhaps, deep down, didn't even want to share.

The shame was insidious, a poisonous vine wrapping itself around my heart and squeezing the life out of my self-worth. It whispered insidious lies in the quiet hours, convincing me that I was somehow responsible, that I had invited the abuse that I was damaged goods, unworthy of love, respect, or even basic human decency. The adults in my life, those who should have protected me, were either oblivious, complicit, or simply overwhelmed by their own struggles to offer any kind of solace or support. This lack of understanding further cemented the silence, creating a wall between myself and the world, a wall built from fear, shame, and a desperate need to protect myself from further pain.

The gay scene, which I was thrust into at an age far too young, added another layer of complexity. It wasn't a safe haven; it was a minefield of exploitation, sex, drugs, alcohol and highly predatory behaviour, masked behind a facade of acceptance, liberation, glitter and sequins.

The very gay scene that accused me of making someone HIV positive when I was at the age of 18. No matter how much I said I was not HIV positive, I had tested Negative, so it couldn't have been me. They didn't care. They wanted to believe the vicious lie, the untruth that destroyed any shred of confidence I had in this insidious scene.

My gay doctor, also an openly gay man on the Townsville scene also confirmed it wasn't me with the person I supposedly infected and I am still HIV Negative to this day, but it was all too late. The gay scene would believe what they wanted to believe, and the lie was much juicier than the truth.

I was all alone again. The vulnerability I carried from the abuse made me an easy target. I couldn't articulate what was happening to me, not even to myself. It was easier to believe that this was the price of belonging, of acceptance in a world that already felt hostile. The confusion was a potent brew of innocence lost, shame, and the desperation to find a semblance of connection in my chaotic life.

The silence extended beyond my own internal world. There was no one I could confide in. Telling my mother would have been unthinkable; her own life was a tempest of instability, and I instinctively knew she wouldn't–couldn't–handle the additional burden. Even if she had been capable of providing support, the fear of her reaction, the potential for judgment or blame, was paralysing.

My father and stepfather were distant figures, both emotionally unavailable and absent from my life. Turning to them for help was a non-starter. Other adults were either the perpetrators themselves or people I felt would dismiss or judge my experiences. My childhood was a series of betrayals, and the idea of confiding in anyone felt like inviting another violation.

The consequences of this prolonged silence were profound. The shame eroded my self-esteem, leaving me feeling worthless and perpetually on edge. I developed a deep-seated mistrust of adults, making it difficult to form healthy relationships. The slightest touch, a casual comment, could trigger flashbacks and a surge of anxiety. Simple acts of intimacy felt tainted, burdened by the weight of past trauma.

School was a battleground, a constant struggle to navigate the social complexities of adolescence while simultaneously battling the demons of my past. I became adept at masking my pain, developing a carefully constructed facade of normalcy that concealed the turmoil raging beneath the surface. I became a master of avoidance, retreating into myself, becoming increasingly isolated and withdrawn.

My relationships were equally fraught. I struggled to connect with others on a genuine level, always fearing exposure and always expecting rejection. I sought intimacy but sabotaged it at every turn, pushing people away before they could get too close, terrified of the vulnerability it required. My self-destructive behaviours became a way to cope, a way to numb the emotional pain. The shame, the silence, and the constant fear of discovery created an invisible barrier between me and any chance of a real connection.

The impact on my self-image was devastating. I viewed myself through the eyes of my abusers, seeing myself as damaged, flawed, a possession to be used and unworthy of love. The internalised shame became a self-fulfilling prophecy, reinforcing negative beliefs and behaviours. I struggled with feelings of worthlessness, inadequacy, and a pervasive sense of being "broken." This negative self-perception permeated every aspect of my life, affecting my academic performance, career aspirations, and ability to form meaningful relationships.

The silence also manifested in physical symptoms. Anxiety attacks became a frequent occurrence, leaving me trembling and breathless. Sleep became a battleground, haunted by nightmares and the relentless replay of traumatic memories. I developed chronic stomach problems, a constant reminder of the gut-wrenching fear and anxiety that had become a constant companion and would often just withdraw from people.

The physical manifestation of the trauma served as a stark reminder of the deep-seated emotional pain that I couldn't, or wouldn't, acknowledge. Looking back, I understand that the silence wasn't a choice but a survival mechanism. It was a way of protecting myself from the overwhelming pain and the fear of further harm. But the cost of that silence was immense. It perpetuated the cycle of abuse, it eroded my self-worth, it damaged my relationships, and it manifested in a myriad of physical and emotional problems.

The path to breaking the silence was long and arduous, fraught with setbacks and moments of doubt. But the journey, while painful, has been transformative. Sharing my story, giving voice to the pain I had carried for so long, has been an act of defiance, a reclamation of my narrative. It has allowed me to reclaim my identity to rewrite the story of my life on my own terms.

The shame still lingers, a faint echo of the past, but it no longer holds the same power and never will. It is a part of my story, a crucial chapter, but not the defining narrative. My journey is a testament to the resilience of the human spirit and the transformative power of breaking the silence. It's a story of healing, finding strength in vulnerability, and ultimately discovering the enduring capacity for hope and love. It's a story of survival, yes, but also a story of thriving against the odds and the telling of it here is a vital part of my continued healing. The scars remain, a visible testament to the battles fought and won, but they are also a reminder of the incredible strength I found within myself to not only survive but to flourish. The journey continues, and each shared word is a step further towards wholeness. The darkness still exists, but it no longer holds the power it once did. The light has begun to shine, illuminating the path forward.

A Glimmer of Hope Seeking Help

The weight of my secrets had become unbearable. For years, I had carried the burden of my past, that heavy cloak woven from shame, fear, and deep self-loathing. The memories, once fragmented and blurry, had begun to coalesce, forming a horrifyingly clear picture of my childhood. The silence, once a protective shield, now felt like a suffocating prison. It wasn't a single event, a sudden epiphany that propelled me towards seeking help. It was a slow, agonising accumulation of pain, a crescendo of suppressed emotions that finally reached a breaking point.

One particularly cold night, huddled beneath a flimsy oversized shirt on the beach, I remember staring at the stars. The vastness of the cosmos contrasted sharply with the claustrophobia of my own existence. The cold seeped into my bones, mirroring the icy grip of fear that had constricted my heart for so long. In that moment, surrounded by the harsh realities of homelessness and the ever-present threat of violence, a tiny spark of hope ignited within me. It was a fragile flame, easily extinguished, but it was there nonetheless. A flicker of possibility, a whisper suggesting that maybe, just maybe, there was a way out.

The catalyst, if I can pinpoint one, was an encounter with a young man named Brian, he called me buddy and saw beyond the hardened exterior I had painstakingly constructed, noticing the haunted look in my eyes, the tremor in my hands. His gentle demeanour, devoid of judgment, created a space for me to tentatively open up to share fragments of my story. He sat beside me, lit up a cigarette, and listened without interruption, his empathy a balm to my wounded soul. He didn't pry, but his presence was a lifeline, a silent affirmation that I wasn't alone.

Brian didn't offer solutions or pronouncements; instead, he provided something far more valuable: friendship, a listening ear, a drive to the national park, a trip to the island, a hand to hold, a sausage roll, an iced coffee and if I was getting grumpy a mars bar and a walk along the beach talking about antlions, the waves and tides he calmed me in a way I never thought possible. This formed an unbreakable bond between us and his support never wavered, even when he saw the nightmares, sadness and anger. I am who I am today because he loved me and helped me unselfishly through the darkness, the alcohol binging, suicide attempts and re-education of my youth. Brian taught me to drive and helped me in many ways. He even suggested at times that I might benefit from talking to someone who could help me process my experiences. He gave me the number of a local crisis hotline and urged me to reach out. That simple act of kindness, that gesture of unwavering support, was the first crack in bringing down the wall of isolation I had built around myself.

The thought of actually calling the Kids Help Line filled me with an overwhelming sense of dread. My mind raced with a torrent of anxiety. What if they didn't believe me? What if they judged me? What if I couldn't articulate the unspeakable horrors I had endured? The fear was paralysing, threatening to snuff out the fragile ember of hope that had begun to glow. But Brian's unwavering belief, support, his gentle encouragement provided the strength I needed to overcome my hesitation.

It took several days and countless moments of agonising indecision before I finally made the call. My hand trembled as I dialled the number, each ring echoing the pounding of my heart. When a woman answered, her voice calm and reassuring, I hesitated, almost wanting to hang up. But the fear of continuing to live in silence, the weight of my unspoken trauma, propelled me forward. I began to speak, my voice cracking and barely a whisper at first, punctuated by long, tearful pauses. It was a difficult, agonising process, a painful excavation of buried memories.

The woman on the other end of the line listened patiently, her voice a soothing presence in the storm raging within me. She didn't interrupt or offer unsolicited advice. She simply listened, providing a safe space for me to unravel my story, one piece at a time. As I spoke, a strange sense of relief washed over me.

The act of sharing my pain was finally acknowledging the atrocities I had endured felt strangely liberating. It was as if a heavy burden had been lifted, though the scars remained. The hotline became a regular point of contact for many months and provided invaluable guidance on developing healthy coping mechanisms. She encouraged me to engage in activities that nurtured my emotional and physical well-being, suggesting techniques such as mindfulness meditation and spending time in nature. These practices provided much-needed respite from the emotional turmoil, offering moments of peace and self-compassion. She also encouraged me to develop healthy relationships to build a support network of trusted individuals who could offer unconditional love and acceptance. The process was slow, painstaking, and often fraught with challenges, but with every step forward, I felt a growing sense of self-worth and empowerment.

The journey wasn't solely about confronting the past but also about building a future. It was about reclaiming my identity and creating a life that was defined by hope, resilience, and self-love. The path to healing was a long and winding one, but with each step, I grew stronger, more confident, and more empowered. The scars remained indelible reminders of the pain I had endured, but they no longer defined me. They served as a testament to my strength, my perseverance, and my unwavering determination to create a life worthy of living.

The glimmer of hope that had ignited in me had grown into a radiant beacon, guiding me toward a future I had once thought impossible. The journey was far from over, but I knew, with absolute certainty, that I was on the right path.

Finding Support and Building Trust with Professionals

The decision to seek professional help was terrifying, a leap of faith into the unknown. For years, I'd built walls around my heart, brick by brick, each one cemented with shame and fear. Breaking them down felt like dismantling my entire being.

My first attempt was with a general practitioner, a kind, older man who'd been my mother's doctor for years. He listened patiently, his gaze unwavering as I stammered through a fragmented account of my childhood. But the sheer enormity of what I was trying to convey felt overwhelming, even for him. He referred me to a local counsellor, a young man with a warm smile and an empathetic demeanour.

The initial sessions were helpful, a safe space where I could begin to unpack some of the less traumatic aspects of my life. However, as I delved deeper into the abuse, I realised he lacked the specialised training to handle the complex trauma I had endured. It wasn't his fault; he did his best, but the unspoken weight of my experiences hung heavy between us, an invisible barrier preventing me from fully disclosing the extent of my suffering.

The search for the "right" therapist felt like searching for a needle in a haystack–a needle I wasn't even sure existed. I went through several therapists, each encountering a gamble, a tentative step forward, often followed by a painful retreat. Some were dismissive, their reactions ranging from subtle scepticism to outright disbelief. Others were well-meaning but lacked the specific expertise to address the multifaceted trauma of childhood sexual abuse. The feeling of being misunderstood, of not being believed, was profoundly isolating and deeply disheartening.

It reinforced the self-doubt that had plagued me for so long, whispering insidious lies in my ear, telling me I was exaggerating, that I was imagining things, that I was unworthy of help.

One therapist, a man with a stern demeanour and a clinical approach, through the Salvation Army Men's Shelter, tried a technique that I found incredibly damaging. He pushed me to confront my memories in a way that felt invasive and triggering, re-traumatising me rather than healing me and the wording, well, what could you have done differently just grated against my soul? The experience left me feeling raw and vulnerable, reinforcing my ingrained fear of trusting others. Another therapist, a woman with a gentle voice and a calming presence, focused solely on the behavioural aspects of my trauma, overlooking the emotional and psychological devastation it had inflicted. Her methods, while well-intentioned, felt superficial and ultimately ineffective.

The process was arduous, a relentless cycle of hope and disappointment. Each failed attempt chipped away at my already fragile sense of self-worth, leaving me feeling more alone and isolated than ever yet again. There were moments when I considered giving up and sometimes months between seeking help when the overwhelming weight of my past threatened to consume me. But something deep inside, a stubborn ember of hope, kept me going. I knew, deep down, that there had to be someone, somewhere, who could help me navigate the labyrinth of my trauma.

I explored other avenues of support. I joined an ad hoc support group for survivors of childhood sexual abuse. I was the youngest there by at least 30 years. This group provided a sense of community and belonging, a space where I could connect with others who understood my experiences and there was free tea, coffee and biscuits. It was incredibly empowering to hear other people's stories, to realise I wasn't alone in my suffering and that there were others who had survived and thrived. But I felt alone in the fact I was the only teenager there.

The shared experiences, the empathy and the mutual support strengthened my resolve and encouraged me to continue my journey of healing. The path to healing has been long and winding, filled with challenges and setbacks. But it's also been a journey of self-discovery, of resilience, and of growth. I learned that finding the right support is critical, that not all therapists are created equal, and that the search for healing can be as challenging as the trauma itself.

However, perseverance is key. The right therapist, the right support system, and a commitment to self-care can make all the difference in the world. My journey is a testament to the power of hope, resilience, and the unwavering belief in the possibility of healing. The scars remain, but they are now a testament to my strength, a reminder of how far I've come, and a symbol of the incredible capacity of the human spirit to overcome adversity.

A growing sense of self-worth, self-respect, and a deep understanding of my own inner strength has replaced the shame and self-loathing. The journey continues, but with each passing day, I am more confident in my ability to live a life free from the shadows of my past. The future I once thought impossible is now within my reach.

The healing continues, but the pain no longer dictates my life. I am the author of my own story, and my chapter is far from over.

Navigating Challenges

The initial attempts to articulate the horrors of my childhood felt like trying to climb an insurmountable mountain, barehanded and bleeding.

The general practitioner, who had known my mother for years, listened with a stoic professionalism that, in retrospect, I now recognise as a necessary coping mechanism. He couldn't possibly have absorbed the sheer weight of my confession in one sitting, not without collapsing under the burden and it certainly didn't help that he had known me my whole life.

His referral to a local counsellor was a vital first step, but it was also a stark reminder of the systemic limitations I would face. The counsellor, while well-meaning and empathetic, lacked the specialised training to address the complex layers of trauma I carried. He dealt with anxiety and depression, common issues, but the deep, ingrained wounds of childhood sexual abuse required a different level of expertise.

The realisation that my initial attempts were insufficient was a crushing blow. It wasn't just about recounting the events; it was about the emotional excavation, the painstaking process of untangling the knots of self-blame, shame, and fear that had bound me for so long. My fragmented narratives, punctuated by silences and tears, lacked the coherence and structure that would allow a less experienced professional to truly understand the extent of the damage. It was as if I was trying to convey a complex mathematical equation using only rudimentary arithmetic. The gaps in my storytelling, the unspoken nuances, and the subtle shifts in my demeanour were all significant pieces of the puzzle that remained frustratingly out of reach.

Trying to explain the insidious nature of the abuse to someone who lacked understanding was like trying to paint a vivid, detailed landscape using only shades of grey. The subtleties of manipulation, grooming, and the normalisation of inappropriate behaviours were lost in translation.

For all his good intentions, the counsellor simply lacked the language to interpret these complex dynamics. It was a deeply frustrating experience, fuelling the familiar feelings of helplessness and isolation. It felt as though I was carrying a heavy, unbearable secret, a burden too immense for anyone to fully comprehend, let alone offer meaningful support.

The next attempt involved a worker from the child protection services. A young man caught my eye in the mall and we connected somehow from a few glances and smiles, he reminded me of Leonardo DiCaprio, a tall, beautiful blonde man with gentle eyes. He approached me and said hello and asked if I was ok, I smiled and said, "Hi," sheepishly.

He said, "Look, I have to go back to work and meet with colleagues. Would you like to meet later when I am finished and we can talk?" He further added, "I work for Children's Services, so I am happy to talk to you about anything and it's all confidential."

I replied, "Ok." Later, we met after he finished work for an iced-chocolate. He explained that while he was in Townsville for work purposes, he admitted that he was a gay man and that meeting me sparked an interest in him to get to know me better. He was very clear with me about differentiating his work-related role from his personal interest in me. I realised that meeting him was something other than providing support to me in a professional capacity but something about him told me that he was very caring and genuine.

We talked for ages, it was like I was talking to a long-lost friend. He asked me if I wanted to go up to the room where he and his colleagues had been conducting their work during the day. I agreed we went up to the room. They were using facilities in the hotel in Flinders Mall. It was a lovely suite; the curtains were drawn, and the lighting was low. We sat on the lounge and I noticed video cameras on tripods and I queried it. He stated that he was working with police in providing training for professionals on how to interview children who had experienced suspected sexual abuse. He said that I should ignore the cameras as they were purely for training purposes. He offered to remove them if that made me feel more comfortable. I said it's ok, I am happy for you to leave the cameras where they are.

We spoke about my whole life. I felt so at ease looking into his eyes. I was so comfortable with him and after several hours, we got closer and we cuddled. He asked if he could kiss me and I said, "Yes." My mind was spinning in a way I had not known for years. We were intimate and I stayed the night without any nightmares and without the fight or flight feelings. He was truly amazing energetically, he had a touch that made me feel comfortable, at ease, truly seen and loved. I had not felt like this with anyone in a very long time. We formed a long-distance friendship. I wanted more for years after this and we had a very open romantic dialogue. We talked for hours, and we even sent each other mix tapes of music, but the distance between us and my horrible self-sabotage tendencies ultimately ended our relationship and he moved overseas, how I wished it was different. He and I continued to have on and off again contact over the years that followed, including to the time of writing this book.

As for a formal investigative process in Townsville, the abuse itself was daunting, a labyrinthine maze of forms, interviews, and assessments. My memories were still fragmented, clouded by years of repression and self-protection. The formal setting, with its sterile atmosphere and impersonal tone, triggered a wave of anxiety that made coherent communication nearly impossible.

The questions felt intrusive, each one a sharp jab reopening already festering wounds. I felt judged, scrutinised, and misunderstood, reinforcing the deeply ingrained belief that I was somehow to blame for what had happened. The investigative process highlighted the stark contrast between the emotional reality of my experience and the systemic requirements for proof. The system demanded concrete evidence and irrefutable facts, but my memories were often hazy, clouded by the trauma itself. The lack of physical evidence or corroborating witnesses made it challenging to build a solid case.

My words, raw and vulnerable, were not sufficient; they were dismissed as unreliable, emotional outbursts from a troubled youth, a narrative often associated with those who had experienced trauma. It reinforced the feeling that my voice and truth held no weight within the system designed to protect those who had suffered similar experiences.

This experience left me feeling deeply alienated and betrayed. The system that was supposed to provide support and justice instead left me feeling more vulnerable and exposed. The lack of validation and understanding intensified my sense of isolation and deepened my self-doubt. It felt like another insurmountable hurdle on my arduous path to healing.

I then sought support from a local support group for survivors of sexual abuse. It was amazing you would often find the best groups listed on notice boards in shopping centres or at the sexual health clinic. This proved to be a more fruitful avenue. Being surrounded by others who understood who had experienced similar struggles, was incredibly powerful. The shared experiences created a sense of community and validation. The group sessions provided a safe space to process my emotions, express my pain, and realise that I was not alone.

The collective healing was powerful and I began to understand that my silence had contributed to my isolation and shame. It was a crucial step in acknowledging the abuse and the effect it had on my life. Yet, even here, navigating the dynamics of the group proved to be challenging. Sharing my story felt intensely vulnerable, even amongst a group of understanding peers. Triggering flashbacks and overwhelming emotional responses in the sessions were common and this heightened the urgency of finding a therapist specifically trained in trauma.

The search for the right therapist was a lengthy and often frustrating process. Many therapists lacked specialised training in trauma-informed care, leading to re-traumatisation during sessions. Some lacked the understanding of the unique psychological complexities of childhood sexual abuse or how easily one could be triggered. Others seemed to lack the emotional capacity to bear witness to the trauma. The constant need to explain and justify my experiences, to constantly prove the validity of my suffering, was deeply exhausting. It felt like running a marathon while carrying a heavy burden. The sheer effort to access appropriate support became a source of trauma in itself.

Finally, through extensive research and referrals, I connected with a therapist specialising in complex trauma and childhood sexual abuse. This proved to be a turning point. The therapist's understanding and empathy were profound. He didn't push me to disclose more than what I was comfortable with and created a safe and supportive environment where I could begin to unravel the complex web of trauma. He provided validation, helping me unpack my feelings of guilt and shame and replacing self-blame with self-compassion.

His expertise provided a framework within which I could process my experiences. It was a gradual process, slow and deliberate, respectful of the pace I needed. His approach was grounded in safety, and this was critically important.

This therapist helped me understand that my experiences were not my fault, that I was a survivor, and that I deserved support. He helped me process my emotions, develop coping mechanisms, and reclaim my narrative. With his guidance, I learned to manage the flashbacks, nightmares, and intense emotions that had plagued me for so long. We worked through the layers of trauma, exploring the various ways the abuse had impacted my life, my relationships, and my sense of self.

The healing wasn't a linear progression. There were setbacks and regressions. There were days when I wanted to give up and return to the familiar numbing of my past. However, I persisted. The therapeutic journey was like reconstructing a shattered vase, painstakingly piecing together fragments of my past, my identity, and my hope.

Navigating the system was a harrowing experience, but it was also a crucial step in my journey to healing. The challenges highlighted the systemic failures in providing adequate support to survivors of childhood trauma, highlighting the urgent need for improved training, resources, and sensitivity within the social services sector.

The journey wasn't easy and there were many times that I felt defeated and alone. However, the persistent search for the right support, the unwavering commitment to self-care, and the resilience that emerged from the trauma itself were instrumental in my journey toward healing. The scars remain visible reminders of the pain I endured, but they are now symbols of my strength, my perseverance, and my unwavering commitment to living a life free from the shadows of my past.

The Power of Therapy Reclaiming Identity

The referral to the local counsellor, while a lifeline of sorts, proved to be a temporary fix. His gentle approach, while comforting, lacked the depth required to unpack the complexities of my trauma. We talked about anxiety, about the nightmares that plagued my sleep, about the pervasive sense of unease that clung to me like a second skin. But the underlying issue, the core wound, remained untouched. He couldn't, or perhaps didn't know how to, delve into the specifics of the abuse. The unspoken hung heavy in the air between us, a barrier of unspoken shame and fear, both his and mine. I felt like I was tiptoeing around the edges of the abyss, never truly confronting the monster that haunted me.

After several sessions that felt more like polite conversations than genuine therapy, I knew I needed a change. The feeling of being misunderstood, of not being truly seen or heard, was almost as painful as the memories themselves. I started researching therapists specialising in trauma, specifically childhood sexual abuse. Finding one who accepted my limited financial resources proved challenging. The waiting lists were long, the costs prohibitive. Yet, the sheer desperation to escape the suffocating grip of my past fuelled my persistence. I scoured online forums, contacted social services again, and even reached out to support groups for survivors. Each phone call and email felt like another small victory in a war against the overwhelming sense of isolation.

Finally, after what felt like an eternity, I found one and his reputation preceded him. He was known for his expertise in trauma-informed therapy and his compassionate approach to working with survivors. The first session with him was different from any I'd experienced before. There was no gentle easing into the conversation, no small talk to build rapport. He looked me directly in the eyes, acknowledging the pain etched onto my face, and simply said, "Tell me your story." so I did. I poured out decades of suppressed anguish, the memories flooding back with a raw intensity that left me breathless and trembling. This time, however, the tears were different. They weren't tears of shame or self-blame; they were tears of release, of finally allowing myself to grieve the innocence that had been stolen from me.

He didn't interrupt or offer platitudes and listened intently and without judgment, providing a safe space for my pain to surface. He validated my feelings, assuring me that what had happened to me wasn't my fault, that I was not to blame and a lot for anyone to navigate. It was a profound revelation, a turning point in my healing journey. For so long, I had carried the weight of the world, believing myself to be somehow responsible for the horrors I had endured. His unwavering belief in my innocence, in my inherent worth, has been a transformative experience.

Our sessions followed a vast array of medications to trial and a structured approach, incorporating several therapeutic modalities. Transcranial Electro Magnetic Stimulation (TEMS) proved particularly effective in helping me process the weight of the Trauma and the memories. The rhythmic stimulation helped refire pathways in the brain, stimulating areas that had been shut down. This has allowed me to access and reprocess those memories in a way that didn't feel overwhelming. It wasn't about erasing the memories—that wasn't possible—but rather about changing their emotional charge. Through TEMS, I started to detach from the intense emotional pain associated with those memories, allowing them to become less debilitating and more manageable.

Cognitive Behavioural Therapy (CBT) helped me challenge the negative thought patterns that had developed as a result of the abuse. For years, I had internalised messages of worthlessness and self-loathing. CBT provided me with the tools to identify and challenge those negative thoughts, replacing them with more positive and realistic ones. I learned to recognise the distortions in my thinking and the ways in which my past experiences had shaped my perception of myself and the world. This process was gradual, a step-by-step dismantling of the self destructive beliefs that had held me captive for so long.

Alongside therapy, I started exploring other avenues of self-care. I discovered the power of meditation, which helped me to regulate my emotions and find moments of peace amidst the chaos.

I started exercising regularly, even though it was only small amounts to start with, as it was difficult for me to sometimes even get out of bed, but finding solace and strength in the physical exertion did make me feel a little better, even if it was walking alone on a beach. The focus on my physical well-being wasn't simply about physical health; it was also about reclaiming control over my body, a body that had been violated and abused for so many years.

The journey of healing was far from linear. There were setbacks, moments of regression, and times when the pain felt too overwhelming to bear. However, with unwavering support from my therapists and friends and the tools I had acquired through therapy, I learned to navigate these difficult periods. I developed a coping mechanism that helped me manage the flashbacks, the nightmares, the intrusive thoughts the darkness calling me to end it all. I also learned the importance of self-compassion, of being kind and forgiving to myself. This was perhaps the hardest lesson of all: to accept myself, flaws and all, to forgive myself for the things I couldn't control, for the pain I had endured.

One of the most significant aspects of my healing journey was the reclamation of my identity. For years, I had defined myself solely by the abuse I had suffered. I believed that my past experiences dictated my present and my future. But, through therapy, I began to reconstruct my sense of self to create a narrative that was not solely defined by trauma. I rediscovered my passions, my strengths, and my inherent worth. I started to see myself not as a victim but as a survivor, a testament to the resilience of the human spirit.

The therapeutic process also involved confronting the shame and guilt that had been ingrained in me since childhood. I had internalised the belief that I was somehow responsible for the abuse, that I had deserved what had happened to me. Through therapy, I challenged these beliefs, learning to understand that shame is a tool of abuse, a weapon used to control and silence victims. By confronting my shame and guilt, I was reclaiming my power, my voice.

The healing process was long and arduous, but it was also incredibly rewarding. It was a journey of self-discovery, of self-acceptance, and of empowerment. Therapy and medication were not a magic cure. It was a tough road, two steps forward and sometimes three steps backward. It was a process of ongoing work, of continual growth and transformation. It wasn't about erasing the past but about integrating it into my life in a way that didn't define or diminish me.

The scars remained, etched into my memory and my being, but they no longer held the power to dictate my life. They were reminders of the pain I had endured but also symbols of my resilience, of my strength, of my unwavering determination to live a life free from the shadows of my past.

My journey to healing was a testament to the power of therapy, to the transformative potential of self-care, and to the enduring strength of the human spirit. It was a journey that taught me the importance of seeking help, finding my voice, and reclaiming my identity, not as a victim but as a survivor. The path wasn't easy, but it was a path worth walking. The journey was one of profound self-discovery, a testament to the healing power of acknowledging, processing, and, ultimately, transcending the deep wounds of horrific childhood trauma. It was a journey that ultimately led me to a place of peace, self-acceptance, and a renewed sense of hope. It was a journey I would not trade, for it forged in me a strength and resilience I never knew I possessed. This is a journey I share, not to dwell on the darkness but to illuminate the path toward healing and the enduring possibility of a life lived fully and freely.

Forgiveness and Self-Acceptance A Long Journey

The therapist I eventually found was different he possessed a quiet strength, a calm intensity that didn't flinch from the darkness. He didn't shy away from the details; he didn't judge. Instead, created a safe space, a sanctuary where I could finally articulate the horrors I had buried deep within. He listened, not with pity, but with empathy, validating my pain and acknowledging the profound impact of the abuse. This wasn't just about talking; it was about unpacking, layer by layer, the intricate tapestry of trauma that had woven itself into the fabric of my being.

Forgiveness, he explained, wasn't about condoning the actions of my abusers. It wasn't about absolving them of responsibility. It was about releasing myself from the shackles of anger, resentment, and the consuming need for revenge that had held me captive for so long.

He used metaphors, relating the anger to a heavyweight I carried, a burden that was slowly crushing me. He encouraged me to visualise letting go, to imagine placing that weight down, feeling the lightness, the freedom that followed.

The process was agonisingly slow. Some days, the anger felt insurmountable, a raging inferno that threatened to consume me. On other days, I felt numb and detached, as if the events were happening to someone else. There were days of intense emotional upheaval, waves of grief and self-loathing crashing over me, leaving me gasping for air. My therapist helped me navigate these turbulent seas, teaching me coping mechanisms and grounding techniques to help me center myself when the storms raged. He introduced me to mindfulness practices, encouraging me to focus on the present moment, to anchor myself in the here and now rather than being lost in the suffocating grip of the past.

Self-forgiveness, he explained, was perhaps the most challenging aspect of the journey. The insidious voice of self-blame, the whispers of inadequacy that had haunted me since childhood, were relentless. I had internalised the shame and guilt, believing that somehow, I had deserved the abuse, that I had been complicit in my own suffering. This internalised narrative needed to be challenged, dismantled, and replaced with a kinder, more compassionate self-perception.

My therapist helped me identify and reframe these negative self-beliefs. He taught me to challenge the validity of those internalised criticisms and question their origins and impact on my present life. He introduced the concept of self-compassion, urging me to treat myself with the same kindness and understanding I would offer a close friend in distress. It felt unnatural at first, almost foreign, to extend such compassion to myself. But with practice, consistent self-reflection and self-care, the seeds of self-compassion began to take root, slowly pushing aside the thorny weeds of self-blame and self-hatred.

The journey towards self-acceptance was a winding path, filled with twists and turns, ups and downs, and moments of profound insight interspersed with periods of agonising doubt and self-questioning. There were days when I felt strong, empowered, and confident in my ability to navigate the challenges ahead. And there were days when the old wounds reopened, when the pain felt fresh and raw as if the years hadn't passed, as if I was still that vulnerable, terrified child.

But through it all, I clung to the hope that I held within. I focused on the progress I had made, on the small victories, on the incremental steps toward healing and self-acceptance. I learned to celebrate those moments of triumph, no matter how small, acknowledging the strength and resilience it took to get there. This consistent self-affirmation helped counter the negative self-talk, the internalised criticisms that threatened to derail my progress.

Forgiving my abusers wasn't about forgetting what happened. It wasn't about erasing the pain or minimising the harm they inflicted. It was about releasing the grip they had on my emotions, freeing myself from the cycle of anger and resentment that had kept me bound to the past. It was about recognising that holding onto that anger was only harming me, preventing me from moving forward and building a life free from the shadows of my past.

The process involved a lot of emotional work. I had to confront the rage, the betrayal, the profound sense of violation. But I also had to acknowledge the humanity of my abusers. Not to excuse their actions but to understand the complex interplay of factors that might have contributed to their behaviour. This wasn't about excusing their crimes; it was about disentangling myself from the narrative of victimhood that had defined so much of my life. It was about reclaiming my power and my ability to shape my own destiny.

This understanding came gradually. It wasn't a sudden epiphany but a very slow, deliberate process of self-reflection and emotional processing. I learned to separate their actions from my inherent worth. I learned to understand that their choices were their own and that their choices did not diminish my value as a human being.

I am worthy of love, respect, of happiness, regardless of the atrocities I endured as a child in Townsville. Self-acceptance is an even greater challenge. It meant confronting the deep-seated insecurities that had taken root in my childhood. It meant acknowledging the lasting impact of the abuse on my self-perception and my relationships. It meant learning to love myself, flaws and all, to embrace the complexities of my own being. It meant recognising that my scars, both visible and invisible, were a part of my story, but they did not define me.

This process involved embracing self-compassion, ecognising that I was not alone in my struggles and that millions of others had endured similar trauma and had emerged stronger on the other side. I started connecting with support groups, finding solace and solidarity in sharing my experiences with others who understood. These connections were invaluable, providing a sense of community, belonging, and a feeling of not being alone in my pain.

The path to forgiveness and self-acceptance is a lifelong journey, not a destination. There are days when the old wounds resurface when the memories return with a jarring intensity. But the difference now is that I have the tools, the coping mechanisms, and the support network to navigate those challenging moments.

I no longer feel overwhelmed by the pain; instead, I acknowledge it, process it, and try to move on.

The journey has been transformative. It has allowed me to reclaim my narrative, rewrite my story, and define myself on my own terms, not as a victim of my past but as a survivor, a testament to the resilience of the human spirit. The scars remain, a permanent reminder of the darkness I endured.

But they are also a testament to my strength, to my unwavering determination to heal, to forgive, and to ultimately accept myself fully and completely. This acceptance, this self-love, is the most precious gift I have ever received, a gift I continue to cultivate and nurture each and every day. This ongoing journey of self-discovery, healing and growth is something I share, not to burden others with my past, but to offer hope and encouragement to anyone else struggling with similar experiences. It is a story of survival, resilience, and, ultimately, of profound peace found within.

A peace that comes from finally acknowledging the pain, forgiving the unforgivable, and embracing the beautiful, imperfect self I am today.

Legal Process

The decision to pursue legal action was not an easy one. For years, the weight of my experiences had been a suffocating blanket, silencing my voice and fuelling a deep-seated sense of shame. The idea of confronting my abusers of reliving the trauma in a formal setting felt utterly terrifying. Therapy has helped me to understand the abuse and to process the emotional damage, but the thought of facing my perpetrators in a courtroom filled me with a visceral fear that threatened to overwhelm the progress I'd made.

My therapist, a compassionate man with years of experience working with survivors of sexual abuse, had gently guided me through the process of considering legal action. He helped me weigh the potential benefits–the possibility of justice, of holding my abusers accountable against the risks–the potential for re-traumatisation, the emotional toll of reliving the horrors.

There were no guarantees, he explained, no promise of a perfect outcome. The legal system, for all its potential for good, is often slow, cumbersome, and emotionally draining.

The initial steps were daunting. Finding a lawyer specialising in cases of childhood sexual abuse was crucial. Many lawyers shy away from such cases, citing the complexities, the emotional investment required, and the often-slim chances of success. Finding someone who understood the nuances of trauma, who was patient and empathetic, felt like finding a needle in a haystack. Eventually, after several consultations that went nowhere, I went to the police the meeting was incredibly difficult. I had to recount my experiences, detailing each instance of abuse in excruciating detail.

Their expression remained neutral, and questions were carefully worded to avoid triggering further distress. It was emotionally exhausting, a relentless wave of memories washing over me, threatening to drown me in a sea of pain and fear. It was a gruelling marathon. I was told I needed proof, witnesses, photos, something to substantiate what had happened. I felt defeated and instantly kicked in the guts. It was hopeless for me. I had left it all too long.

Normally, there would be depositions, interviews with investigators, and countless hours spent reviewing documents and preparing for potential court appearances and that is all before it gets to court.

The legal system is notoriously slow, months, even years, can pass between hearings and court dates, the uncertainty exacerbating anyone's anxiety and sense of powerlessness.

The thought of not being able to face my abusers in the courtroom was perhaps the most difficult thing I had to come to terms with.

Yet, there was an odd sense of closure. Just the process of talking through everything at this level provided a formal mechanism for validating my experiences. It had given a voice to the silenced child within. I felt an overwhelming weariness, a sense of emptiness that threatened to engulf me once again.

This time, I was determined that I would not let it consume me. The strong support network I had cultivated enabled me to approach this with a different kind of strength and resilience.

I found therapeutic outlets to express myself and find meaning. The journey wasn't over, but the sense of a long road travelled with hope for a better future had begun. This stage taught me to appreciate the delicate balance between justice and healing.

Facing Abusers Confrontation and Closure

What truly started the healing was the subsequent unplanned encounters, or rather, near encounters. The first was at the local supermarket. I saw him—one of my abusers, Uncle Larry, a man whose face I'd tried to erase from my memory but whose presence still triggered a visceral reaction. He was older now, his hair greying, and his features softened over time, but the recognition was instant and overwhelming.

My breath hitched in my throat, my heart pounded a frantic rhythm against my ribs. For a moment, I was paralysed, frozen in the aisle, the fluorescent lights humming a discordant tune to the tremor in my hands. Then, a wave of anger—raw, potent anger I hadn't realised I possessed—washed over me. It wasn't the all-consuming rage I'd imagined; instead, it was a quiet, burning intensity, a controlled fire.

I didn't approach him. I didn't scream or shout. Instead, I simply turned and walked away, my steps measured deliberately. The feeling wasn't one of fear, not anymore. It was a sense of empowerment, a quiet victory. It was the moment I realised I was no longer the frightened child he had preyed upon. I was a survivor, and I was strong. I allowed myself the luxury of feeling safe enough not to act on the primal urge to retaliate. At that moment, he ceased to be a terrifying monster and became just...a man. An ordinary man with the weight of his actions hanging heavy upon him, a man who I knew I no longer had to fear. That moment of self-preservation control was a significant step on my path to healing.

After I moved away from Townsville to a different State for over 30 years, I decided to move back to Queensland to Brisbane in the suburb Annerley in 2022 and in an ironic twist, I discovered that Larry also lived in Annerley and is a tour guide working with young and old alike at a tourist hotspot. I do wonder if these places even do police checks on people. I guess, given it was back in the 1960's when he was incarcerated, it's probably fallen off any basic police check for a job or possibly there is a different story in regards to his incarceration.

Another time, I saw another abuser, Tony, a former family acquaintance. My mother and stepfather went to visit him for some reason. I suspect it was to borrow money. This was a different kind of encounter. This encounter sparked a different kind of emotion. Unlike the supermarket incident, where controlled anger reigned supreme, this one ignited a complex cocktail of emotions. The initial shock of seeing him open the door gave way to a wave of sadness, a profound sadness for the child I once was, for the innocence that had been so brutally stolen. But I stood there standing tall and yet Tony seemed smaller than my memory portrayed him, age and time had stripped some of his power away. I didn't speak to him. I didn't need to. His look of horror when he saw me with them was golden, worried I might say something to his wife or my mother. He could barely look at me, the simple acknowledgement of his presence was enough. It wasn't a confrontation but a confirmation: I had survived. I was here, I was whole, and his actions, however devastating, no longer held the power to define me but obviously haunted him.

This encounter brought forth a wave of sadness. Sadness for the innocent child I had once been. It was a profound sadness, a feeling that carried within it the painful weight of those lost years and experiences. This sadness deep in the pit of my stomach, while intense, was different from the debilitating despair I had carried for so long. This sadness was productive, a crucial component in my ongoing healing. The sadness was the acknowledgment of the pain I had gone through, yet I held this emotion without being consumed by it and I didn't let him see it.

When I was 16, I was down at a local beach in Townsville called Shelley Beach with a dear old friend, Chloie. Chloie was a much older man but had a heart of gold towards me we were just friends. We would sit on the balcony of his house and drink tea and eat rice pudding and talk about life or we would go for a drive in his yellow Suzuki Jimny to the beach and sunbake and talk for hours. He would tell me about all the different people that would come along and who to avoid, as Chloie had been around for a long time and knew everyone.

He pointed out one older man he called Sheepdog, Bob because he used to relentlessly only chase after young boys. Chloie told me to keep clear of him at all costs. A few hours later, Chloie decided he needed to leave and go home, but I stayed as I loved the beach. It was a sanctuary and escape for me and kept my mind calm.

Shortly after Chloie left the beach, the other man, whom I was told to avoid, approached me and said, "I know you. You're Nancy's boy, Joey."

I looked at him strangely and asked, "How do you know that?"

He replied, "I used to babysit you."

My mind literally went into a panic and instant fight or flight mode. This man was Robert, the first person to sexually abuse me as a child at the age of 7. I told him to leave me alone and go away. He refused to leave, so I packed my bag and started walking away. He followed me and I started saying louder, "Go away, leave me alone, stop following me."

He didn't and kept following and getting closer. He kept saying, "Let's talk. Let's talk." I didn't want to talk, so I just ignored him. He approached me quickly and grabbed my arm and said, "Come on, let's go into the bushes and play around."

I pushed him away and said, "No! Fuck off." He grabbed me again and tried to kiss me. I was fighting him off, we struggled and he pushed me into the creek at the end of Shelly Beach and jumped in with me, he grabbed me, I was terrified as firstly I couldn't swim and I had a phobia of being in water where I couldn't see the bottom or what was in there with me and this was crocodile country.

I was pushing him off me, yelling get off me, let me go fuck off, get off me he was grabbing me and trying to get my shorts off and trying to touch my penis. I kept pushing him and hitting him and swearing at him to get off me. I got my arm free and I punched him right in the face. It shook him enough that he let me go. I got away from him, crawled out of the creek, and ran away from him down the beach. I only saw him 2 times after that on the beach on different occasions, but he knew not to come anywhere near me, and he never did after that.

I consider myself very lucky to have had the strength to get away from him that day. If I had been weak, it's possible I could have been abused again or worse, abused and drowned in a creek and left for the crocodiles to hide their sins.

The last encounter was seeing Prior, the man that brutally beat and raped me while his friend Jarred watched when I was a child. I was at the Townsville Show with my friend Brian and all of a sudden, out of the crowd, walked a man with a group of Indigenous friends. I stopped and froze with fear, while my abuser, Prior, did not see me or notice me, I certainly noticed him. This encounter rocked me to my very core. I had a panic attack and Brian was so worried for me, so we left and went home.

That night, Brian witnessed me have a nightmare and once I woke, he consoled me and held me through this traumatic experience. We talked about it in great depth and I realised that my abuser didn't need to have this control over me. I needed to control my own resilience, self-acceptance and love, knowing what happened was tragic, but again, it did not define me and I had to confront my feelings and that would empower me.

Brian said walking away was the best thing I could have done, even though he still wanted me to go to the police. I didn't because I had done that years prior and it didn't go anywhere. These encounters, or rather the near encounters, became a form of silent confrontation, a declaration of my resilience, my reclaiming of my narrative. I didn't seek revenge. Instead, I found a different kind of justice: the quiet assertion of my own strength. It wasn't enough to simply identify the pain.

The real work was in understanding its roots, in tracing its origins back to the source, the initial trauma. This wasn't simply an intellectual exercise. It was an emotional journey, often painful and disorienting but ultimately liberating. It was a process of piecing together the shattered fragments of my identity, of reclaiming the parts of myself that had been stolen, lost, or buried deep within. It was about finding my voice. Finding the courage and strength to speak my truth.

The process also involved confronting the societal narratives that often surround childhood trauma. The narratives that blame the victim place the responsibility on the abused. The shame, the guilt, the self-blame–these were burdens I carried for many years. But through therapy, I began to recognise these as insidious constructions, as tools of oppression designed to silence survivors. I learned to separate their words and actions from my self-worth, a critical step in my healing.

The healing journey was also about self-compassion, a profound and necessary act of self-love. For years, I'd been exceptionally harsh on myself, critical of my shortcomings and failures. I learned to replace this self-criticism with self-acceptance and understanding, to treat myself with the same kindness and compassion I would extend to a cherished friend. This self-compassion wasn't about minimising the pain I'd experienced or ignoring the challenges I faced; it was about acknowledging my wounds and nurturing my healing.

The healing process is deeply personal and unique to each individual, and there is no limit to the time frame for recovery. What works for one person may not work for another. There's no single path, no magic bullet. But one thing is certain: healing is possible. It's a long, challenging journey, but it's a journey worth taking. The reward is a life lived fully and authentically, a life freed from the shackles of the past, a life brimming with hope and resilience.

My encounters with my abusers, or the near encounters, were not moments of violent confrontation but rather silent affirmations of my survival. They weren't about revenge, but about reclaiming my power, recognising the resilience within, and acknowledging the profound and lasting impact of trauma, not as a defining factor of my identity but as a part of my narrative. The journey to healing is a testament to the inherent strength and capacity of the human spirit to overcome unimaginable adversity.

There is no single definition of closure. For some, it might be a formal apology; for others, it might be a sense of acceptance and understanding.

For me, closure came not in a single, dramatic event but in a gradual process of healing, self-discovery, and empowerment. It was in those unplanned encounters, in the quiet strength of my departure, in the recognition of my own resilience. It was in the acceptance that while the past remains a part of me, it no longer defines me. It is a story that has helped shape me and inform me, but it does not dominate who I am.

The scars remain but are a testament to my journey to the strength I discovered within myself. They are reminders of the pain I have endured but also a testament to the profound capacity for healing and resilience that resides within the human spirit. There are marks of survival, etched into my soul, but they are not the definition of who I am. I am more than my past. I am a survivor. I am resilient. And I am whole.

Dealing with the Aftermath

My social life, already tenuous, crumbled further. I opened up to a very dear family friend, Michelle Kennedy (Deceased). Michelle had known me all my life and she struggled to understand the depth of my pain and the complexities of my emotional state. She simply didn't know how to support me as she knew three of the people who abused me. She was angry and overwhelmed by the enormity of my story and it affected her own mental health issues. Michelle and her lovely partner told me I could stay with them if I ever needed to stay. They didn't have a bedroom for me, so Michelle closed in her carport with shade cloth and put in a single bed for me to sleep on. I was grateful and stayed there for about two weeks. However, Michelle's emotional state was fragile, and I eventually left. And this led to a painful feeling of even greater isolation as I loved her as family.

My ability to connect with people in general and those with their own emotional trauma was a struggle for me. I did not have the ability to fully comprehend or be able to process others' mental health issues and I struggled to be vulnerable and open, as my emotional development was altered and my emotional regulation and understanding were severely hampered in many ways from my childhood.

People in the Gay Community shunned me and pushed me away, made up cruel stories about me if I refused to sleep with them or rejected them, and guaranteed the following weekend, there would be another story about the infamous Joey. Anything from being a thief to damaging cars to being a gold digger, they eventually created and believed a lie so big that it made me leave my hometown for over 20 years.

Therapy provided a safe space to explore the intricate relationship between my past and my present. It helped me to understand how the trauma had shaped my perceptions, my behaviours, and my relationships. It helped me recognise the patterns of self-sabotage and the ways in which I unconsciously recreated the dynamics of my abusive past in my current life. This self-awareness was essential in breaking free from the cycles of trauma.

Through therapy, I began to understand the importance of self-compassion. For so long, I had internalised the shame and guilt associated with the abuse, believing that I was somehow responsible for what had happened to me. Therapy helped me challenge these destructive beliefs to replace self-blame with self-acceptance and self-forgiveness. This was a crucial step in my healing journey.

It was the first step in accepting myself, flaws and all, without the burden of self-recrimination. The therapeutic process also involved reclaiming my narrative. For years, my story had been dictated by my abusers, the dead ends of justice and my silence, a testament to their power over me.

Therapy gave me the opportunity to rewrite my story, to reclaim my voice, and to articulate my experiences on my own terms. This was a powerful act of self-empowerment.

Sharing my story, first with my therapist and eventually with others, became a vital component of my healing. It was a way to reclaim my agency and transform my suffering into a source of strength. Even now, years later, the echoes of the past still reverberate within me, and they always will. The scars remain, both visible and invisible. But the scars are no longer symbols of defeat; they are a testament to my strength, perseverance, and capacity for healing. They are reminders of the pain I have endured but also a testament to the profound capacity for healing and resilience that resides within the human spirit. They are marks of survival, etched into my soul, but they are not the definition of who I am. I am more than my past. I am a survivor, I am resilient, I am loved, I am whole.

My healing continues a daily practice of self-care, self-love, and unwavering self-belief. The journey is long and arduous, but

I walk it with renewed strength, supported by the lessons I've learned, the resilience I've discovered, and the unwavering hope that I will continue to thrive. My story is not just one of survival but of transformation, of reclaiming my life, and of finding joy and peace even amidst the enduring scars of my past.

It's a testament to the profound capacity for healing that resides within each of us, a reminder that even in the darkest of times, hope and resilience can prevail. It is a story of healing, not just for myself but for anyone who has ever felt the crushing weight of trauma and for anyone who carries the burden of a broken past. This is my story–a testament to the incredible capacity of the human spirit to heal, overcome, and find a path toward wholeness and peace.

Processing Trauma Through Writing

My dear friend Meryl, a beautiful woman with kind eyes and a gentle soul, suggested writing. Not just jotting down notes but truly writing. She encouraged me to explore the swirling emotions, the fragmented memories, the unspoken words that had haunted me for so long.

At first, the idea felt daunting, almost impossible, so I pushed it to the back of my mind. One afternoon she took me to a news agency and picked up a blank writing book and said you need to start writing, the number of times I picked up the book and put it down with nothing in it was uncountable. How could I possibly translate the darkness I carried into words? How could I even begin to articulate experiences that felt so utterly devastating?

The first attempts were clumsy, stilted, filled with gaps and inconsistencies and sometimes just a list of random words, people and places. My hand would tremble as I clutched the pen, the ink smudging across the page, mirroring the blurring of my own memories. Sentences would trail off, incomplete, lost in the labyrinth of my trauma. There were days when I couldn't write a single word, paralysed by the sheer weight of what I needed to confront. On other days, the words poured forth in a torrent, a desperate attempt to exorcise the demons that had held me captive for so long.

I started with fragments, snippets of memory, and images rather than narratives. The smell of stale cigarette smoke and cheap beer clinging to the room where it happened. The chilling touch, the cold sweat beading on my skin. The taste of dust and despair, the bitter tang of violation. These seemingly insignificant sensory details held the power to unlock entire chapters of my past, transporting me back to moments I had tried so hard to forget.

Gradually, the fragments began to coalesce, forming the rudimentary skeleton of a narrative. I wrote about the chaotic environment of my childhood, the constant instability, and the absence of safety and protection. I described my mother's struggles, not to excuse her failings but to understand them within the context of her own pain and limitations.

It wasn't then nor now do about blame, and I worry about how she would feel if she read this, but it was about piecing together the shattered fragments of my history, creating a coherent narrative from the chaos of my life.

Writing became a form of excavation. Each sentence I wrote was a shovelful of earth removed, revealing layers of buried emotions and memories. There was immense pain, of course, the raw anguish of remembering. But there was also a surprising sense of empowerment, a feeling of regaining control. For years, my story had been defined by the actions of others by the violence inflicted upon me. Now, I was the one shaping the narrative, choosing the language, and selecting the focus.

I wasn't just recounting events; I was interpreting them, making sense of them, and assigning meaning to experiences that had previously felt meaningless and random. I explored the complex emotions that accompanied the trauma–the shame, the fear, the anger, the self-loathing. I learned to name these emotions, acknowledge their presence, and understand their role in shaping my life. This process wasn't always comfortable, but it was necessary. The words themselves became tools for understanding, providing a framework for processing emotions that had been bottled up for years.

The act of writing this allowed me to confront my own complicity, the ways in which I had unconsciously perpetuated the cycle of abuse. I wrote about my self-destructive behaviours, the ways I had sought validation in unhealthy relationships, and the ways I had allowed myself to be exploited. This was perhaps the most challenging aspect of the writing process, forcing me to confront aspects of myself that I had previously avoided. But the acknowledgement of these patterns was crucial to breaking free from them.

As my writing progressed, I began to notice shifts in my perspective. The shame and self-blame that had been so pervasive began to dissipate, replaced by a growing sense of self-compassion. I started to see myself not as a victim but as a survivor, someone who had endured unimaginable hardship and emerged stronger. The writing process allowed me to re-evaluate my past to separate the actions of others from my inherent worth.

The act of sharing my story giving voice to my experiences, proved incredibly powerful, breaking down the walls of isolation that had surrounded me for so long.

My writing helped me to develop a greater understanding of the issues that contributed to my trauma. I learned about the prevalence of child abuse, the societal factors that perpetuate it, and the inadequate support systems available to victims. This understanding fuelled my desire to write this to help prevent others from experiencing the same pain I had endured.

The writing process became more than just a therapeutic exercise; it became a form of self-discovery, a means of reclaiming my identity, and a testament to the resilience of the human spirit. It was a journey of confronting the darkest aspects of my past while simultaneously celebrating the unwavering strength I found within myself.

The scars remain visible and invisible, but they are no longer the defining features of my life. They are markers on a path of healing, resilience, and, ultimately, wholeness. They are reminders of the pain I endured but also of the incredible strength I found within myself to navigate through the darkness and into the light. The writing was, and remains, a vital part of this continuous process, a testament to the power of self-expression and the enduring capacity of the human spirit to heal and overcome. It is a process that continues, a testament to the ongoing journey of self-discovery and a reminder that even the deepest wounds can eventually begin to heal.

The journey is long and winding, but the destination, a life lived fully and freely, is worth every step of the way. This writing, this sharing, this journey of healing, is a gift I continue to give myself, a testament to the resilience that lies dormant within us all, waiting to be awakened. It is a beacon of hope, illuminating a path forward for myself and for others who walk a similar road. It is a testament to the indomitable human spirit and its remarkable capacity for healing.

The Importance of Support Systems

My journey wasn't a solitary trek through the wilderness of trauma; it was a shared pilgrimage sustained by the unwavering support of others. Without the network of individuals who extended their hands, offered their shoulders to lean on, and simply listened, I highly doubt I would be here today. The healing process, as I discovered, is not a solo endeavour. It's a collaborative effort, requiring a village of individuals willing to walk alongside you, offering comfort, guidance, and unwavering belief in your capacity to heal.

One of the most crucial elements of my support system was the unexpected strength I found in long-term friendships. These relationships deepened in ways I could never have anticipated. Friends who had known only fragments of my story became anchors in the storm, offering solace, understanding, and a much-needed sense of normalcy in a life that had been anything but. Their willingness to listen, without judgment, to my painful stories, their patient acceptance of my emotional fluctuations, and their simple acts of kindness—a phone call, a shared meal, a comforting hug, a drive up a mountain—provided the essential emotional sustenance I needed to navigate the darkest hours. These friendships weren't without their challenges.

There were times when I pushed them away, overwhelmed by shame and self-doubt. There were times when my pain felt too heavy to share, too raw to expose. But my friends, to their immeasurable credit, remained steadfast. They didn't force me to share more than I was ready to; they simply offered their presence, their unwavering support, their silent understanding.

This patient acceptance was, in itself, a powerful form of healing. It validated my experience, assuring me that my pain was real, that my feelings were valid, and that I wasn't alone in my struggles.

The unexpected support of my younger brothers proved crucial. This wasn't the case across the board; my family history was complex and fraught with its own traumas and dysfunctions. But amidst the wreckage of my past, some family members emerged as beacons of light.

My little brother Tim and his partner Ariel unexpectedly offered their home as a safe haven when I was struggling, and they both did multiple 9-hour drives with their family to check in on me. They provided not only shelter but also a quiet sense of acceptance, a refuge from the chaos that had characterised my life.

Their kindness was a lifeline, a reminder that not all family relationships were tainted by the darkness of my past. Their actions were a powerful testament to the redemptive power of unexpected compassion.

The importance of professional support can't be overstated. Therapy provided a safe space to process my trauma, to confront my pain without judgment, and to develop healthy coping mechanisms. It was a long and often arduous process, but it proved to be an essential component of my recovery.

The therapeutic process wasn't simply about processing past trauma; it was also about building a stronger, healthier sense of self. Through therapy, I learned to identify my strengths, recognise my resilience, and develop a more positive self-image. This was crucial, as years of abuse had left me feeling worthless and broken. Therapy helped me reclaim my sense of self-worth to redefine my identity outside the confines of my past experiences. It provided me with the tools I needed to rebuild my life and create a future free from the shadows of my past.

The support I received wasn't always consistent. There were times when I felt utterly alone when the weight of my trauma seemed unbearable. There were periods of isolation and despair where the support systems I had built felt distant and unreachable. But even during these challenging periods, the memory of kindness and compassion from others, the echo of their words of encouragement, sustained me. These memories became internal resources, reminding me that I wasn't truly alone, that there were people who cared and who believed in my ability to heal, even when I struggled to believe it myself.

The importance of a strong support system cannot be overemphasised. It's not simply about having people around; it's about having individuals who understand, empathise, and offer unwavering support without judgment. It's about having a safe space to process emotions, to share experiences, and to build a stronger sense of self. It's about accepting help, recognising your own limitations, and acknowledging that healing is a journey that's best travelled with others alongside.

My healing journey was a winding path, filled with unexpected detours and unforeseen challenges. There were setbacks and regressions, moments of despair and doubt. But throughout it all, the unwavering support of friends, family, and professionals provided the essential scaffolding that enabled me to navigate the turbulent waters of my trauma. Their compassion, understanding, and unwavering belief in my resilience were the life rafts that kept me afloat when I felt ready to sink.

The scars of my past remain visible and invisible. But they no longer define me. They are reminders of the pain I endured but also of the incredible resilience I found within myself and the extraordinary power of human connection in the face of adversity.

My story is a testament to the transformative power of support, a beacon of hope illuminating the path toward healing for others who walk a similar road. It is a story of survival, resilience, and the enduring strength of the human spirit, a testament to the remarkable capacity for healing when we allow ourselves to accept the support we need.

It is a message of hope, a reminder that even in the darkest of times, there is always light to be found, often in the most unexpected of places, and always in the unwavering support of those who stand by our side and, ultimately, that support, that connection, is what allows the journey from shattered innocence to reclaimed wholeness to begin.

Rebuilding Trust and Relationships

Rebuilding trust wasn't a single act but an extremely slow, painstaking process, like piecing together a shattered mirror. Each shard represented a broken connection, a betrayal, a violation of innocence. The initial years after escaping the immediate clutches of my abusers were a blur of therapy sessions, medication adjustments, and the constant, nagging feeling of being watched, even when I was alone. The world felt like a menacing place, full of potential threats, and every interaction was fraught with anxiety. Simple acts of kindness felt suspicious, gestures of friendship calculated. My default setting was mistrust, a protective mechanism honed by years of abuse.

My relationships with authority figures, a complex mix of fear and resentment, were particularly challenging. The police, social workers, and even my therapists, while ostensibly there to help, were figures of the system that had largely failed me in the past. The fear of being judged, of being disbelieved, of being further victimised created an almost insurmountable barrier. I found myself constantly second-guessing their motives, interpreting their actions through a lens warped by past experiences. It took time, immense patience, and a willingness to be vulnerable with the right people to begin to dismantle these walls.

It started subtly. A social worker who listened without judgment, who didn't pry or push, who validated my feelings without offering empty platitudes. A therapist who understood the nuances of complex trauma, who didn't rush the process, who allowed me to set the pace. These were the individuals who started to chip away at the hardened exterior I had built to protect myself. They didn't demand trust; they earned it through consistent empathy, genuine concern, and a steadfast commitment to my well-being. Their actions spoke louder than any words.

With professional support, I began to understand the insidious nature of my mistrust. It wasn't simply a reaction to past abuses; it was a deeply ingrained survival mechanism, a learned behaviour that had become a part of my identity. Therapy helped me unpack these layers of emotional baggage, identify the triggers that set off my anxiety, and develop coping mechanisms to manage my responses.

Cognitive Behavioural Therapy (CBT) was particularly helpful in challenging the negative thought patterns that fuelled my mistrust. Learning to recognise and reframe these thoughts was a gradual process, but it slowly allowed me to see the world with a more balanced perspective.

Building healthy relationships with peers was equally daunting. Initially, I clung to isolation, afraid of intimacy, convinced that closeness would inevitably lead to betrayal. The thought of letting someone get close enough to hurt me was terrifying. The idea of vulnerability felt like a death sentence. I built walls, both physical and emotional, keeping people at arm's length, afraid of being exposed, of being discovered as the damaged person I was.

Overcoming this fear required a conscious effort to step outside my comfort zone. It started with small steps—joining a support group for survivors, attending social gatherings with a trusted friend, and engaging in online forums with other individuals who understood my experiences. These small acts of bravery, though often anxiety-inducing, were crucial in gradually expanding my circle of trust. In these spaces, I found a sense of community, a shared experience that validated my feelings and reduced the crushing weight of isolation.

Finding people who understood my experiences and didn't judge or minimise my trauma was invaluable. These individuals offered a safe space to share my story, to process my emotions, and to gradually let down my guard. In their acceptance, I found a sense of belonging, a validation that I had not previously experienced. These relationships, though forged in the crucible of shared trauma, became sources of strength and support. They offered a stark contrast to the toxic relationships of my past.

Another significant aspect of rebuilding trust involves setting boundaries. This was something I really struggled with, conditioned as I was to acquiesce to the demands of others, even when it meant compromising my well-being. Learning to say "no," to assert my needs, and to protect my emotional space was a transformative experience. It was a process of reclaiming my autonomy, taking control of my life and defining my own terms of engagement. The fear of upsetting others was slowly replaced by a growing self-respect.

This process also involved carefully evaluating new relationships, being mindful of red flags, and recognising patterns of manipulative behaviour. This wasn't about becoming cynical or distrustful but about developing a healthy sense of self-preservation.

It was about learning to recognise my own worth and to choose relationships that aligned with my values and nurtured my well-being. I learned to prioritise my emotional health over the approval of others.

Developing romantic relationships was particularly challenging. Years of abuse had left me with a profound sense of unworthiness and a distorted sense of self. Intimacy felt like a risk, a potential vulnerability that could be exploited, and sexual intercourse had no real feelings attached to it. It was just going through the motions. Sometimes, I would have sexual intercourse with random strangers just to see if I could feel anything emotionally, but I rarely did. When I did, I fell for them very hard and that, in turn, would trigger all my issues with self-sabotage and paranoia to kick in.

The fear of repeating past patterns of abuse was ever-present. It took significant self-work and therapeutic support to unravel these deeply ingrained beliefs. Learning to love myself, to accept my imperfections, and to trust that I deserved healthy, reciprocal relationships was a long and arduous journey.

My first attempts at romantic relationships were tentative, cautious, and often fraught with deep anxiety. I found myself constantly overthinking, analysing every interaction, and searching for signs of potential harm. I just wanted to keep them, I would become possessive and defensive and I couldn't get close enough. These early experiences, though sometimes painful, were important learning opportunities. They helped me identify my own emotional triggers, refine my boundaries, and develop strategies for navigating the complexities of intimacy.

As I gained confidence and self-awareness, I became better at choosing partners who respected my boundaries, who valued my well-being, and who understood the impact of my past.

The journey of rebuilding trust and forming healthy relationships is ongoing. It's a process that requires constant vigilance, self-reflection, and a willingness to address past traumas. There will be setbacks, moments of doubt, and instances where my trust is challenged. But with the support of my therapist, my support network, and a growing understanding of myself, I am increasingly confident in my ability to navigate these challenges. The scars remain, but they are fading. They serve as a reminder of the strength I discovered in the face of unimaginable adversity. They are also a testament to the transformative power of healing and the possibility of building a life filled with genuine connection and lasting love. This is not the end of my story but the beginning of a new chapter, one filled with the promise of a brighter future.

Educational and Professional Pursuits

The initial steps towards a formal education felt monumental. After years of instability and interrupted schooling, the very idea of a classroom seemed alien and intimidating. The casual cruelty of some classmates, the subtle snickers and sidelong glances were a constant reminder of my past vulnerability.

I was a walking paradox: a young adult burdened with a child's emotional baggage, attempting to navigate a system designed for those with stable and supportive childhoods. My initial attempts at community college were marked by anxiety attacks and feelings of profound inadequacy. I struggled to concentrate, plagued by flashbacks and intrusive thoughts. The simple act of raising my hand in class felt like a betrayal, a confession of my damaged past.

My dear friend Brian taught me to acknowledge my past without being defined by it and to see my struggles not as failures but as opportunities for growth. To look at education and TAFE as little steps to becoming a better person to be able to give myself the opportunity to thrive again.

This was a gradual process, a slow rebuilding of my self-worth and confidence. I discovered the power of supportive relationships at TAFE, a small group of like-minded students who were understanding of my difficulties and supportive of my healing journey, provided a vital network of encouragement. These individuals, initially hesitant and cautious, gradually became my friends. They saw past my emotional scars and recognised my inherent potential.

Their acceptance was a powerful antidote to years of rejection and isolation, proving that genuine connection and trust were possible, even after enduring such profound betrayals. Their belief in me, often more robust than my own, was essential to my persistence.

One particularly challenging aspect was managing the financial burden of education. The precariousness of my early life had left me with little financial security. I worked casual jobs while attending classes, often sacrificing sleep and personal time. The juggling act between studies, work, and therapy was exhausting, but the determination to build a better life for myself fuelled my perseverance.

There were moments of desperation when I seriously considered abandoning my studies, succumbing to the overwhelming pressure. But the memory of the abuse, the pain I had endured, kept me going. It served as a reminder of how much I wanted to escape the life I had known, a testament to the unwavering desire for a future free from the shadow of my past.

My academic journey wasn't ideal. There were setbacks, moments of doubt, and times when I felt overwhelmed by the challenges. There were classes I failed, exams I barely passed, and assignments that felt insurmountable. But each failure became a lesson learned, a chance to refine my strategies, and a test of my resilience.

I learned to approach my studies with a greater sense of self-compassion, recognising that perfection was an unattainable ideal. I discovered the importance of self-care, of setting boundaries, and of prioritising my mental and emotional well-being. These newfound skills proved invaluable, not only in my academic pursuits but also in navigating the complexities of my daily life.

Eventually, I earned my Certificate 3 in Hospitality and sometime after then on to do two Certificates in Property and finally a Degree in Property in both Queensland and Victoria, all while working full-time in the industry, a milestone I celebrated with a quiet sense of triumph. The accomplishment was not merely academic; it was a personal victory, a testament to my resilience and determination. It marked a significant turning point in my journey of healing and self-discovery.

The sense of accomplishment went beyond the academic validation; it was a powerful affirmation of my inherent capacity for growth and change. This was not just an achievement; it was a testament to years of hard work, perseverance against overwhelming odds, and a profound commitment to building a brighter future.

Inspired by this success, I am now considering continuing my education by enrolling in a program in Social Work, Counselling and Psychology or Nursing. The choice stems from a deep-seated desire to help others who have endured similar experiences.

I wanted to offer support and guidance, to provide a lifeline to those lost in the darkness of trauma, as I had been. My personal journey became the driving force behind my professional aspirations. My experiences, though painful, had gifted me with an exceptional level of empathy and understanding.

A diploma in social work, psychology, counselling or nursing will be my next endeavour and will be very demanding, requiring a delicate balance between theoretical knowledge and practical application. Internships will provide invaluable hands-on experience working with vulnerable populations. I will learn about trauma-informed care, the complexities of the child welfare system, and the multifaceted challenges faced by individuals navigating the aftermath of abuse.

I hope to work with children and families, offering support, guidance, and a safe space to process their pain. While this work will be emotionally taxing, I believe it will be deeply rewarding to use my experiences to support others. The professional world to date has presented its own unique set of challenges. Trauma from being overworked, under-supported, targeted and victimised to the point of leaving the Property Industry and workforce for a period of time.

My own personal vulnerability created moments of self-doubt and anxiety, and the betrayal and lies of managers to save the company from a major scandal topped it all off. There were times when I felt overwhelmed when the weight of it all threatened to derail my progress. However, the tools and strategies learned through therapy, coupled with the strong support system I had cultivated, provided a solid foundation for resilience. I have developed healthy coping mechanisms to manage workplace stress and created boundaries to protect my emotional well-being.

I hope my future professional path will lead me to a non-profit organisation dedicated to supporting survivors of childhood sexual abuse. This will allow me to directly impact the lives of others who have endured similar hardships. I hope to provide counselling and support, creating a safe and validating environment for individuals to share their stories and begin their journeys of healing. This will be a constant reminder of the power of resilience, the transformative potential of human connection, and the possibility of rebuilding lives shattered by trauma.

Finding Stability and Independence

Leaving the suffocating grip of my past wasn't a sudden, dramatic break. It was a painstakingly slow climb, a series of small victories meticulously stacked upon each other. The first step was finding a safe space, a haven where the echoes of my past wouldn't haunt me at every turn. This meant escaping the transient, chaotic existence that had defined my childhood. Finding a stable place to live was more challenging than it sounds. Landlords, understandably wary of my age and lack of a consistent employment history, often turned me away. The fear of ending up back on the streets, back in the vulnerable position that had allowed my abuse to flourish, was a constant, gnawing anxiety. It fuelled my determination.

I eventually secured a small rental property in a quiet part of Townsville, far removed from the familiar haunts of my past. The rent was manageable, thanks to the part-time job at Cactus Jacks Restaurant I'd managed to secure. It wasn't glamorous, slinging fries and clearing tables, but it offered a sense of normalcy, a routine that anchored me to the present. The mundane tasks – the rhythmic sizzle of the grill, the clinking of plates, the polite exchanges with customers – became a form of self-soothing.

They were predictable, manageable, and a stark contrast to the unpredictable chaos of my past. The money wasn't much, but it was enough to cover rent and food, allowing me to finally breathe a sigh of relief, free from the constant, crushing weight of financial instability. Building a support network was equally crucial. The isolation I had endured throughout my childhood had been a significant contributor to my vulnerability. Now, I actively sought out connections, albeit cautiously.

I started attending support groups for survivors of abuse, a daunting but ultimately life-changing decision. The initial vulnerability felt almost unbearable; the act of sharing my story of articulating the horrors I had endured felt like tearing open old wounds. Yet, within the shared experiences of others, I found a sense of community, a sense of belonging I had never known before. Listening to the stories of other survivors, stories so similar to my own, was both heartbreaking and empowering. It validated my experiences, confirming that I wasn't alone and that what happened to me wasn't my fault.

Education became another avenue of empowerment. The initial attempts at Hospitality College had been fraught with anxiety, but I persisted. I developed strategies to manage my anxiety, like taking regular breaks, practicing mindfulness exercises, and seeking support from academic advisors. Slowly, cautiously, I began to thrive. The act of learning, expanding my knowledge and skills, became a powerful antidote to the feelings of helplessness and worthlessness that had haunted me for so long. I found a deep sense of purpose in my studies – a sense of control over my life that had previously been absent. My academic success became a tangible symbol of my resilience, a testament to my determination to overcome the challenges of my past.

There were setbacks and moments of profound despair when the weight of my past threatened to overwhelm me. There were days when the nightmares returned with brutal intensity, days when the flashbacks left me paralysed with fear. But I learned to navigate these difficult moments, to rely on the support system I had carefully built. My friends were my anchors during the storms, reminding me that I wasn't alone, that I was strong, and that I could overcome these challenges. Graduating my studies marked a significant milestone, a culmination of years of hard work, perseverance, and unwavering belief in myself. The ceremony wasn't just a celebration of my academic achievement; it was a celebration of my survival, a testament to the incredible strength I had discovered within myself. It was a public acknowledgement that I had not only survived but had thrived, transforming the pain of my past into a force for positive change.

My journey from victim to survivor, from a child marked by trauma dedicated to healing, hasn't been easy. It has been a long and arduous climb, filled with obstacles and setbacks, moments of profound despair. But it has also been a journey of extraordinary growth, resilience, and self-discovery. I have learned the profound importance of self-compassion and the power of forgiveness, not just for others but for myself.

I have discovered a strength I never knew I possessed, a resilience that has allowed me to not only survive but to thrive. Most importantly, I have found purpose, meaning, and a deep sense of fulfillment in helping others navigate their own journeys towards healing and recovery.

My scars remain a permanent reminder of the pain I endured, but they are also a symbol of my strength, my resilience, and my unwavering commitment to making a difference in the world. They are badges of honour, testaments to my survival and my triumph over adversity.

In sharing my story, I hope to offer hope and inspiration to others who have walked a similar path, reminding them that healing is possible and that even the darkest of nights can give way to the dawn. The future may hold more challenges, but I face them with a newfound confidence, knowing that I possess the strength and resilience to overcome them. My journey is a testament to the indomitable spirit of the human heart, its capacity for healing, and its ability to find beauty and purpose even in the face of unimaginable pain.

Awareness Giving Back

The act of sharing my story wasn't solely about providing relief from repressed emotions it was about a profound shift in perspective. For years, my trauma felt like a shameful secret, a heavy burden I carried alone. The silence, the fear of judgment, the insidious whisper of self-blame – these were my constant companions.

But as I began to piece together the fragments of my shattered childhood, a new understanding dawned. My pain wasn't unique; it was a shared experience, a pervasive darkness that touched countless lives. This realisation ignited a fire within me, a fierce determination to challenge the silence, to break the chains of shame, and to become a voice for those who couldn't find their own.

The path to providing this wasn't straightforward. Initially, the very idea terrified me. The vulnerability it required felt overwhelming, the potential for re-traumatisation a constant threat. I wrestled with the fear of reliving the horrors I had endured, of being confronted by the same scepticism, disbelief, and blame that I had encountered for so long. Would people believe me? Would my story be dismissed as sensationalism, exaggeration, or simply a fabrication? The anxieties were crippling at times, yet the desire to help others outweighed my fear.

Sitting amongst other survivors, listening to their stories, was simultaneously agonising and profoundly validating. Hearing echoes of my own experiences in their words – the shame, the confusion, the isolation helped me to understand that I wasn't alone in my suffering. It also fuelled my resolve to make a difference. The women and men in that group, brave in their vulnerability, showed me that healing was possible and that even in the deepest darkness, hope could bloom.

My role evolved from listener to active participant. I began to share my own story, cautiously at first often withholding detail, then with increasing confidence. Each time I spoke, a piece of the burden was lifted. Each time I connected with another survivor, a sense of empowerment grew. The power dynamics shifted; I was no longer a victim defined by my past but a survivor, a beacon of hope for others. My experiences, once sources of shame and humiliation, transformed into tools of healing and empowerment for others.

One particularly memorable experience involved working with a pregnant young woman who had been repeatedly abused by a family member. She was trapped in a cycle of silence, fear, and self-blame, convinced that she was somehow responsible for the abuse. Through compassionate support, I helped her to challenge these deeply ingrained beliefs, to reclaim her voice, and to understand that she was a victim of a horrific crime, not a perpetrator. Seeing her gradually regain her self-worth and find a path towards healing was profoundly rewarding.

The challenges remain significant. The stigma surrounding child sexual abuse persists, hindering open conversations and delaying the process of healing for many survivors. Funding for support services continues to be inadequate, leaving many individuals without access to essential care. Legislative loopholes still exist, allowing perpetrators to escape accountability. The fight for justice is far from over. But seeing the resilience of survivors has instilled in me an unwavering hope for a future where all children are safe, survivors are supported, and perpetrators are brought to justice.

This journey has been a deeply personal one, a testament to the power of healing and the transformative potential of forgiveness. It has also been a journey of profound gratitude — gratitude for the support I received along the way, the opportunities that allowed me to grow and thrive, and the privilege of serving as a voice for others. My scars are a reminder of the pain I endured, but they are also a source of strength, a symbol of my unwavering commitment to making a difference in the world one person at a time by sharing my story, I hope to offer hope, inspiration, and a message of healing and resilience to others who have walked a similar path.

The future remains uncertain, but I face it with newfound confidence, knowing that I possess the strength and resilience to overcome any obstacle. My journey is a testament to the indomitable spirit of the human heart, its capacity for healing, and its ability to find beauty and purpose even in the face of unimaginable pain. The fight for healing continues, and I remain committed to being a part of that fight. The wounds may never fully heal, but the spirit of resilience remains unbroken.

The Importance of Self-Care and Continued Healing

The initial euphoria of escaping the clutches of my past didn't last. The scars, both visible and invisible, remained. The nightmares, though less frequent, still clawed at the edges of my sleep. The lingering anxiety, a constant, low hum beneath the surface of my days, was a stark reminder of the fragility of my newfound peace. Building a new life wasn't a single, momentous event; it was a relentless process of rebuilding, brick by brick. The crucial element in this reconstruction was self-care, a commitment to nurturing my physical, emotional, and spiritual well-being.

This wasn't about pampering or indulging in fleeting pleasures. It was about developing a consistent, proactive approach to managing my trauma's lingering effects. It started with the basics: To-do lists, mantras, regular sleep patterns, regular exercise, and a good diet. I often fell off the bandwagon, but I always jumped back on. These weren't just buzzwords; they were vital tools in my arsenal against the insidious creep of depression and anxiety.

For years, my body had been a vessel of abuse, neglected and violated. Now, I had to relearn how to treat it with kindness, respect, and care. Regular exercise became my meditation, a way to release pent-up tension and reconnect with my physical strength. It wasn't always easy. Some days, the thought of putting on running shoes felt insurmountable. But I learned to listen to my body, honour its limitations, and celebrate even the smallest victories. A 15-minute walk became a triumph.

My diet underwent a similar transformation. For so long, food had been a source of comfort, a way to numb the pain. Now, I consciously choose nourishing foods, fuelling my body with the nutrients it needs to heal. This wasn't about restriction or deprivation; it was about mindful eating and appreciating the sustenance that fuelled my recovery. I started to notice the connection between the food I ate and how I felt, both physically and emotionally. I discovered the power of healthy fats to nourish my brain and the calming effect of herbal teas.

Beyond the physical, I had to address the emotional and spiritual wounds. Therapy was, and continues to be, an indispensable part of my healing journey. It provided a safe space to process my trauma, to unpack the layers of pain and confusion, and to confront the insidious narratives of self-blame and shame that had taken root in my mind. My therapist wasn't a magic wand, waving away my pain. Instead, they were a skilled guide, helping me navigate the treacherous terrain of my memories and emotions. We explored coping mechanisms, strategies for managing anxiety and triggers, and ways to cultivate a healthier sense of self.

There were setbacks, moments of intense emotional distress, and days when I felt like giving up. But the support of my therapist, along with my growing network of friends and family, helped me navigate those challenging moments. Learning to identify and manage my triggers became crucial. Certain smells, sounds, or situations could send me spiralling back into the darkness. Through therapy, I learned to recognise these triggers, develop coping strategies, and gradually lessen their impact. This involved deep breathing exercises, mindfulness techniques, and grounding exercises that helped me reconnect with the present moment when feeling overwhelmed.

Another crucial aspect of self-care was fostering healthy relationships. For years, my relationships had been characterised by instability and toxicity. Now, I consciously sought out supportive, healthy connections. This involved setting boundaries, communicating my needs clearly, and surrounding myself with people who valued and respected me. This wasn't always easy. Trust was a hard-earned commodity, and the fear of vulnerability lingered. But gradually, I learned to trust again, to open my heart to others, and to cultivate relationships built on mutual respect and understanding.

The spiritual aspect of self-care was equally vital. I explored different spiritual and philosophical practices, seeking solace and meaning in the face of immense suffering. Meditation and spending time in nature became essential components of my self-care routine. These practices helped me connect with a sense of peace and stillness, a counterpoint to the chaos and turmoil of my past. They allowed me to cultivate a sense of inner strength and resilience, enabling me to face the challenges of my present with greater equanimity.

Forgiveness, a concept often misrepresented as condoning the actions of abusers, became another crucial component of my healing journey. It wasn't about absolving my abusers of their responsibility; it was about releasing the burden of anger and resentment that had consumed me for so long. Holding onto that anger was a poison, slowly eroding my spirit.

Forgiving them, however, didn't erase the pain; it allowed me to reclaim my power and move forward. It allowed me to reclaim the narrative of my life, shaping my future rather than being defined by my past. The journey toward self-care and continued healing is an ongoing process, not a destination. It's about cultivating a lifelong commitment to nurturing my well-being, a constant vigilance against the insidious return of old patterns and traumas.

There will inevitably be setbacks, moments when the darkness threatens to engulf me. But the tools and strategies I've developed over the years—therapy, mindfulness, healthy relationships, and a commitment to self-compassion—provide a solid foundation for navigating those difficult moments. My scars remain, but they are now badges of honour, testaments to my resilience and capacity for healing.

They remind me of the pain I endured, but they also remind me of the incredible strength I discovered within myself. They are a reminder that even from the deepest darkness, hope can emerge, and a new life can be built, one carefully chosen, self-nurturing step at a time and that is the most profound lesson I have learned.

Healing is possible, resilience is a strength to be cultivated, and a life of peace, purpose and joy is achievable, even after unimaginable adversity. It's a life built not on forgetting but on remembering, on integrating the past into the present, and forging a future grounded in self-love, compassion, and unwavering belief in one's own capacity to heal and thrive. The path is long and winding, but the destination – a life free from the shackles of the past – is worth every step.

Overcoming Trauma: A Testament to Human Strength

The journey recounted in these pages is not one of easy victories or quick fixes. It is a testament to the enduring power of the human spirit, a testament to the capacity for healing even in the face of profound and pervasive trauma. My personal story, as harrowing as it is, ultimately shines a beacon of hope. It demonstrates that the scars of childhood abuse, while indelible, do not define the entirety of one's life. They can, in fact, become a catalyst for profound personal growth, a springboard to resilience, and a foundation for a life lived with purpose and meaning.

My early years, as you have seen, were far from idyllic. The instability, the poverty, and the constant fear were the building blocks of my young life. But amidst this chaos, a certain resilience flickered. I have learned to adapt, to survive, to find pockets of joy in the midst of despair. This innate capacity for survival, this tenacity of spirit, would become my lifeline as I navigated the increasingly treacherous waters of sexual abuse.

The abuse itself, as described in previous chapters, was horrific and devastating. Each incident chipped away at my sense of self, leaving me feeling violated, betrayed, and utterly powerless. The perpetrators, individuals I should have been able to trust, exploited my vulnerabilities, my innocence and my desperate need for love and belonging. The shame and secrecy surrounding the abuse compounded the trauma, creating a profound sense of isolation and loneliness.

Yet, even amidst the darkness, there were glimmers of light. Small acts of kindness, moments of connection, instances where someone offered a helping hand—these fleeting moments provided solace and hope, fuelling my determination to survive.

These were the seeds of resilience that would eventually blossom into a powerful force for healing. The path to healing was arduous and complex. It was not a linear progression but rather a winding road filled with setbacks, breakthroughs, and moments of profound self-discovery. Therapy played a crucial role, providing a safe space to confront the trauma, to process the emotions, and to begin the long process of rebuilding my sense of self.

My therapeutic journey involved facing painful memories, confronting deeply ingrained feelings of shame and guilt, and learning to trust again. My experience highlights the importance of seeking professional help. The skilled guidance of a therapist provided a framework for understanding the trauma, identifying unhealthy coping mechanisms, and developing healthier strategies for managing emotions and navigating relationships. The therapist's role extended beyond simply providing a listening ear; it was about creating a safe space, building trust, and guiding me toward a healthier understanding of myself and my experiences. The therapeutic techniques varied, adapting to my needs and progressing throughout my journey. Cognitive Behavioural Therapy (CBT) helped me to challenge negative thought patterns and develop more adaptive coping strategies. Trauma-focused therapies, such as TEMS (Transcranial Electro Magnetic Stimulation), really helped to be able to pick up the pieces of my life and reduce the emotional impact.

The journey of healing wasn't solely confined to the therapy room. It also involved forging new relationships and building a supportive network of friends and family who understood and accepted me unconditionally. The support I have received from these individuals played an indispensable role in my recovery, providing me with a sense of belonging, validation, and unconditional love. These relationships offered a counterpoint to the damaging relationships of my past, providing stability, fostering trust and helping me to build my confidence and belief in human connection.

Importantly, my journey also involved a process of self-forgiveness and self-acceptance this has not been easy. This was perhaps the most challenging aspect of my healing as I wrestled with feelings of shame, guilt, and self-blame.

Learning to forgive myself for the choices I made as a child, for the ways in which I tried to cope with the unimaginable pain I had endured, was a crucial step toward reclaiming my identity and building a positive sense of self-worth. This wasn't a simple process; it involved acknowledging the impact of the abuse on my perceptions, challenging self-critical thoughts, and developing self-compassion. I have learned to accept that I was a victim, not responsible for the actions of my abusers.

Beyond the personal journey of healing, my story becomes a powerful narrative about the importance of breaking the cycle of abuse. My experience underscores the urgent need for preventative measures for educating children and adults about the signs of abuse and hidden dangers from within family circles and for creating supportive environments where children feel safe to speak up.

My willingness to share my story is a testament to the power of speaking out, of breaking the silence that allows abuse to thrive. By sharing my deeply personal story, I hope to empower others to do the same, fostering a community of support and understanding.

I am dedicated to supporting others and raising awareness necessary to prevent future abuse. My engagement in speaking out and wanting to support others reflects a powerful transformation from victim to advocate.

My dedication to helping others throughout my life underscores my resilience not only in overcoming personal trauma but in turning that trauma into a force for positive change in the lives of others. My contribution extends beyond my own healing, demonstrating the transformative power of turning personal adversity into a story that I hope will benefit the broader society.

The final chapter of this book emphasises that a fulfilling life is possible, even after the most traumatic of experiences. While the scars of abuse may remain, they do not dictate the trajectory of one's life. Healing is possible, and a life filled with joy, purpose, and connection is within reach.

This book concludes not with a sense of finality but with a loud message of hope and empowerment, a reminder that resilience is not simply a trait; it's a capacity that can be cultivated and strengthened through perseverance, self-compassion, and the unwavering support of others.

My journey, however challenging, is a testament to the incredible strength of the human spirit and a powerful reminder that healing is always possible. It provides a beacon of hope, a testament to the remarkable human capacity for resilience, recovery, and, ultimately, a fulfilling and meaningful life. I hope my story will be a powerful catalyst for positive change, offering a message of hope to other survivors and advising the societal changes for preventing further abuse. The journey is long, but the destination, a life free from the shadow of trauma, is attainable.

Breaking the Cycle of Abuse

My own journey toward healing has led me to a profound understanding of the critical need for awareness, prevention, and education at all levels.

While my story focuses on the devastating effects of my abuse, it's equally crucial to address the proactive measures we can take to protect all children and break the cycle of trauma. This is not merely about reacting to abuse; it's about creating a world where such horrors are far less likely to occur.

The first step involves educating children about their bodies and boundaries. This isn't about sexualising them but empowering them with the confidence, vocabulary and understanding to recognise inappropriate touch and behaviour. Simple, age-appropriate conversations about personal space, consent, and the difference between "good touches" and "bad touches" can be incredibly impactful.

We need to teach children that their bodies belong to them, and no one has the right to violate that ownership. This education should begin early, be integrated into regular conversations, and be tailored to the child's developmental stage. It's not a one-time talk but an ongoing dialogue that evolves with their growth. Open communication is key; a child who feels comfortable talking to their parents or caregivers about anything is less likely to suffer in silence.

Beyond the individual child, we must foster strong, supportive family environments no matter the orientation or make of the parental structure. The presence of a nurturing, stable home where children feel loved, valued, and safe is perhaps the most effective preventative measure. Parents and caregivers need to be vigilant, aware of their children's interactions and relationships, and actively involved in their lives.

This doesn't equate to constant surveillance but rather a mindful presence, a consistent willingness to listen, and a genuine interest in their child's well-being. It involves creating a home where children feel comfortable sharing their thoughts and feelings without fear of judgment or retribution.

Open communication channels are crucial for fostering trust and enabling early intervention if anything concerning arises. However, many children don't have access to such supportive home environments. For them, strengthening community support networks is essential.

Schools, community centres, and youth organisations can play a vital role in providing safe spaces, positive role models, and educational programs about child safety. Educating teachers, social workers, and other professionals who work with children about recognising the signs of abuse and how to respond appropriately is critical.

Mandatory reporting laws are in place for a reason; these professionals are often the first line of defence in identifying and protecting vulnerable children. Equipping them with the knowledge and resources to act effectively is non-negotiable.

Early intervention is another crucial aspect of prevention. If a child displays behavioural changes, such as sudden withdrawal, anxiety, fear, or changes in sleeping patterns, it's crucial to investigate further. These could be indicators of underlying issues, including abuse. It's crucial to approach such situations with sensitivity and care, avoiding accusatory language and focusing instead on creating a safe space for the child to express their feelings.

Professional help should be sought promptly through therapists, counsellors, or other child protective services. Early intervention can minimise long-term harm and help prevent further abuse. Furthermore, the societal attitudes towards child abuse must change and that's not just child abuse towards females. It is child abuse to any child, male, female, transgender or those yet to decide. It is a broader issue.

We need to dismantle the culture of silence and shame that often surrounds abuse, creating a climate where reporting is encouraged, not stigmatised. Open conversations about child sexual abuse, without sensationalising and definitely not minimising the issue, are critical in raising awareness and challenging the societal norms that allow abuse to flourish.

This requires a multifaceted approach involving public awareness campaigns, educational initiatives, and a commitment from both government and community organisations to combat the problem.

It means challenging the stereotypes that often surround victims, understanding the complexity of the issue, and acknowledging that abuse can happen in any family, regardless of socioeconomic status or social standing.

Addressing the underlying causes of child abuse is also paramount. Poverty, domestic violence, substance abuse, and lack of access to mental health services and the lack of keeping sexual predators properly monitored are all risk factors that contribute to the incidence of abuse. By implementing comprehensive social policies that address these root causes, we can create a more protective environment for children.

This involves providing accessible and affordable healthcare, including mental health services, investing in family support programs, and addressing issues such as poverty and domestic violence.

Addressing systemic inequalities is crucial in breaking the cycle of abuse. In addition to these preventative measures, we must also focus on creating genuine judgment-free connections and support for children. No one wants to find a 15-year-old child hanging from a tree due to a lack of support networks for survivors.

Survivors need free access to therapy, not just a 10-visit mental health care plan, legal assistance, and other resources that can help them process their trauma and rebuild their lives. Support groups can provide a vital sense of community and shared experience, empowering survivors to choose life, move forward and find healing. Creating a culture of empathy and understanding, rather than judgment and blame, is crucial in fostering a supportive environment for survivors. The long-term impact of childhood sexual abuse is profound, and I know that all too well, it has required a lifetime of work and ongoing support.

Furthermore, we must acknowledge and address the significant role that the internet and technology play in facilitating child sexual abuse. Online predators use the internet to groom and exploit children, and it's critical to equip children, parents, and caregivers with the knowledge and tools to protect themselves online.

This includes education about online safety, the use of parental control tools, and the importance of reporting any suspicious online activity. The internet should be a resource for education and connection, not a breeding ground for abuse. The collaboration between law enforcement, technology companies, and child protection organisations are crucial in combatting the online sexual exploitation of children.

Breaking the cycle of abuse is a complex undertaking, requiring a multifaceted approach that addresses both individual and societal factors. There is no easy fix or a single solution; rather, a collaborative effort involving families, communities, professionals, and governmental agencies is necessary.

My journey, as painful as it has been, has also been a long journey of healing and has become a catalyst for action in my life. The hope is that by sharing my story, we can create a world where fewer children experience the horrors of abuse and where survivors are supported in their journey towards healing and resilience.

The fight against child sexual abuse is a collective responsibility, requiring ongoing vigilance, education, and a steadfast commitment to safeguarding the well-being of all children. The goal is not simply to prevent abuse but to cultivate a world where every child feels safe, loved, and empowered. This is not just a hope; it's a necessary and achievable goal.

Resources and Support for Survivors

The journey out of the darkness isn't a solo trek. It's a path walked alongside others who understand, who offer a hand, a listening ear, and unwavering belief in your strength. For years, I navigated the aftermath of abuse in isolation, convinced that my experiences were unique, shameful, and irredeemable.

I was so close to ending it all on more than one occasion. I gave everything I owned away, I bought people gifts, I acted happy when I was numb and on autopilot, and the biggest lie I told was, *I'm Ok* when I was far from it.

One thing that saved me was my boy Marcus, of whom I am fiercely protective. He is the love of my life. I took him on at 7 weeks old and he is now in high school. He has kept me grounded and stable and is the one thing that has the power to pull me out of the darkness when I feel alone. The truth is, I was far from alone. Millions of individuals carry the scars of childhood trauma, and countless resources are available to help mend those wounds. This isn't about erasing the past; it's about empowering you to build a future free from the grip of that past.

This section is a guide, a map to navigate the complex landscape of support systems available to survivors of childhood trauma and abuse. It is not an exhaustive list—the specific organisations and resources available will vary depending on your location and circumstances—but it's a starting point, a lifeline in the often-overwhelming task of seeking help. Remember that finding the right support can take time and exploration.

Don't be discouraged if the first resource you try isn't the perfect fit or turns you away. Keep searching until you find the people and places that resonate with you—this is very important. Your healing journey is uniquely yours, and you deserve to find support that understands and validates your individual experience.

Let's begin with the most readily accessible resources: helplines and crisis hotlines. These services provide immediate support during moments of distress. Often staffed by trained professionals, these lines offer a safe and confidential space to express your feelings, receive guidance, and develop a crisis plan.

In Australia, the 1800 RESPECT hotline 1800 737 732 offers 24/7 support for people experiencing sexual assault, domestic violence, or family violence.

My favourite was the Kids Helpline 1800 551 800 is another crucial resource providing confidential support for young people aged 5 to 25.

These services are crucial lifelines, offering immediate support during moments of crisis and providing a safe space to begin processing your trauma. Remember, reaching out is a sign of strength, not weakness.

Beyond Blue 1300 224 636 is a confidential service offering counselling support for anxiety, depression and related disorders.

Lifeline 13 11 14 This is a 24-hour helpline.

Police Link 13 14 44 This is a 24-hour helpline.

There's a vast network of organisations dedicated to supporting survivors. These groups offer a variety of services, including individual and group therapy, support groups, legal assistance, and advocacy. Many organisations specialise in specific types of trauma, offering tailored support to meet diverse needs.

For instance, organisations such as Bravehearts focus specifically on preventing child sexual abuse and supporting survivors.

Bravehearts 1800 227 831 support line for adult survivors or sexual abuse.

They offer a multitude of programs, resources, and support tailored to children, young people, and adults affected by child sexual abuse. Your local community likely has similar organisations dedicated to supporting survivors, offering various forms of therapy and support networks. Your local sexual health clinic can also give you a lot of information on organisations in your area that can assist you.

Therapy is often a cornerstone of the healing process. Finding a therapist who specialises in trauma-informed care is essential. These therapists are trained to understand the specific impact of trauma and utilise approaches that prioritise the survivor's safety, empowerment, and control.

Trauma-informed therapy might involve techniques like (TEMS) Transcranial Electro Magnetic Stimulation, (EMDR) Eye Movement Desensitisation and Reprocessing, (CBT) Cognitive Behavioural Therapy or somatic experiencing. These methods address the emotional, psychological, and physical manifestations of trauma, helping to dismantle the negative beliefs and coping mechanisms that have developed as a consequence of the abuse.

It's crucial to find a therapist you feel comfortable with and whose approach resonates with your needs and healing style. Remember that the therapeutic relationship is a partnership, and your feelings and preferences are paramount in the healing process.

Alongside professional therapy, support groups can provide invaluable support. Connecting with others who understand the nuances of childhood trauma can be deeply validating and empowering.

These groups offer a safe space to share experiences, process emotions, and build a community of support. In these groups, you're not alone; you're surrounded by individuals who 'get it,' who can offer empathy and understanding without judgment.

The shared experience often fosters a sense of belonging and helps break the isolation that often accompanies trauma. Emotional validation and camaraderie within a support group are indispensable tools in the recovery process. Many organisations mentioned earlier also facilitate these groups, or you can search for local groups online or through community centres.

Self-help resources, while not a replacement for professional help, can complement therapy and support groups. Books, workbooks, and online resources offer practical tools and techniques for coping with trauma, managing symptoms, and building resilience.

Many books delve into specific trauma types, offering guidance tailored to individual needs. For example, there are self-help resources that focus on PTSD, complex trauma, and the specific challenges faced by survivors of sexual abuse. Always approach these resources critically, acknowledging that they are not a substitute for professional guidance. They can, however, empower you to take active steps in your healing journey by equipping you with practical tools and strategies for self-management.

Legal avenues are also available for those who seek justice or protection and not everyone chooses this avenue and that's ok. Depending on the circumstances, survivors may be able to pursue legal action against their abusers. This can be a complex and emotionally challenging process, requiring the support of legal professionals specialising in this area.

It is absolutely crucial to seek legal advice early on to understand your rights and the potential legal options available to you. In many countries, there are specialised legal services that focus on assisting survivors of abuse and navigating the legal system.

Remember that seeking justice doesn't always equate to a desire for retribution; it can be a way to reclaim power and accountability. This route requires careful consideration and the support of a strong legal team. Prevention is also crucial. As a survivor, I know firsthand how vital it is to create a world where children are protected and empowered.

Supporting organisations dedicated to child sexual abuse prevention empowers future generations, preventing more trauma. These organisations work to educate communities, raise awareness, and advocate for policies that protect children. Their work is not just about responding to abuse; it's about fostering a culture where children feel safe, seen, and heard. By engaging with and supporting these initiatives, you actively participate in building a safer future for children everywhere.

Finally, remember that healing is not linear. It's a journey with its ups and downs, its setbacks and breakthroughs. There will be days when the pain feels overwhelming, and there will be days when you feel a sense of peace and progress.

Be patient with yourself, celebrate your victories, and don't be afraid to ask for help when you need it. Your resilience is remarkable, and your strength is undeniable. You have survived unimaginable adversity, and you are worthy of healing, happiness, and a life free from the shadows of your past. The resources listed above are tools to support you on this journey. Remember, you are not alone, and your healing is possible. Embrace the hope and let the journey of resilience begin.

Finding Your Voice Sharing Your Story

For a long time, the silence was my prison. The shame, the fear, and the sheer overwhelming weight of what I had endured kept me locked in a solitary confinement of my own making. I believed my story was too dark, too shameful, too uniquely horrific and raw to ever be shared. Who would want to hear it? Who would believe me? And more importantly, what good would it do to unleash those memories, to rip open those old wounds?

It has taken decades to find the courage to write this, and I still worry about how reading this will affect my family and friends.

Today, I called my mum and told her what I was doing I advised it may upset her as it is very graphic in parts, so if she wishes me to skip those parts, I will. She said no, I felt my stomach sink and I thought, *Ok this will be tough.*

She said, "It's ok. I want to know everything." I took a deep breath and exhaled and did it again and then I started reading aloud to her and my little brother Matthew, stopping every chapter to see if she was ok or wanted me to make any changes, but she said no, "It's ok."

Mum then said you are my first-born son and I love you no matter what. I want you to know I am proud of you and I know how hard this would have been for you. I love you and I will support you in this. She continued to say she had no idea how to be a mother because of her young age, but she tried. I asked if she wanted me to remove any parts, and she replied NO, this book is the truth, and if it helps you or one other person in the world in any way, then you have my support.

This is the love of a mother, unconditional love and support. I didn't think I would ever tell my mother about my childhood abuse and what happened or my view on my childhood, as it is very raw and would have been very confronting and difficult to hear. I did not want to hurt her in any way. I am glad I finally found the courage to speak up and talk to her, as a huge weight has been lifted off my shoulders for opening up to her after all these years.

The act of sharing my story like this and finally giving voice to the voiceless parts of myself became the removal of the keystone that held the walls of my self-imposed prison. It was a slow, painstaking process, a hesitant whisper that gradually grew into a stronger, surer voice. It wasn't about seeking pity or validation; it was about reclaiming myself and taking back the power that had been stolen from me.

The initial steps were terrifying. I started small, sharing snippets of my experiences with trusted friends and family members. The response was overwhelmingly sad but also positive. Instead of judgment, I received empathy, understanding, and a profound sense of connection. I realised I wasn't alone in my pain. Others had walked similar paths, had endured similar horrors, and had emerged, scarred but unbroken, on the other side. Their stories, their resilience, and their strength became a lifeline for me.

This realisation was a turning point. It fuelled my desire to share my story on a larger scale. I began to explore the various avenues available for sharing trauma narratives. This wasn't about sensationalising my experiences or seeking notoriety; it was about fostering healing, breaking down the stigma surrounding child abuse, and seeking to inspire hope in others.

Writing this book itself is a testament to the power of sharing. The act of putting my personal and graphic experiences into words and meticulously documenting the details of my trauma was empowering. It was like excavating a buried treasure, carefully uncovering the painful fragments of my past, cleaning them, and arranging them into a coherent narrative.

The process wasn't easy; there were days when the memories were so overwhelming that I had to stop, cry, hide in my bed, eat 1 Liter of ice cream and allow myself to grieve, to process the raw emotions that surged to the surface again. But with each word, with each completed sentence, I felt a sense of release, a growing feeling of control over my own story.

Sharing your story doesn't mean you have to expose every detail of your trauma. It's about finding the right level of vulnerability that feels safe and empowering for you. You can start small, sharing fragments of your experience with trusted friends, family members, or a therapist.

My dear friend Meryl told me I might find journaling helpful; writing down your thoughts and feelings can be a powerful way to process your trauma and find your voice. She gave me a book to start journaling, and here we have it, it turned into this book. Consider joining a support group where you can connect with others who understand what you've been through and that your thoughts are normal for what you have been through and there are ways to help find and ground yourself again. The shared experience can be deeply validating and healing.

The therapeutic process itself can be a powerful tool for finding your voice. A therapist can provide a safe and supportive space for you to explore your experiences, process your emotions, and develop coping mechanisms. They can also help you to identify and challenge negative self-beliefs that may be hindering your healing. Therapists who specialise in trauma understand the complex and often-delayed effects of childhood trauma and can guide you through the healing process with patience and understanding.

Consider exploring creative expression as a way to share your experience. Art, music, poetry, and writing can all be powerful tools for processing trauma and finding your voice. These mediums allow you to express yourself in ways that words alone cannot capture. They can also be a powerful way to connect with others who may not fully understand the specifics of your trauma but can still appreciate the beauty and strength of your artistic expression.

Remember, there's no right or wrong way to share your story. There's no pressure to tell everyone everything. The goal isn't to shock or garner sympathy; it's about reclaiming your narrative, finding your voice, and empowering yourself to heal. Your story is unique and valuable, and sharing it can be a profound act of self-love and self-care.

It's crucial to find a safe and supportive environment to share your story. This might involve choosing carefully who you share with, ensuring that those individuals are capable of offering empathy and understanding rather than judgment or dismissal. Consider a therapist or counsellor trained in trauma-informed care as a particularly safe and supportive option. They provide a professional context where your vulnerability is honoured and protected.

Beyond individual support, there are numerous community resources specifically designed to help survivors of childhood trauma. Support groups, online forums, and advocacy organisations offer a sense of community and connection, allowing you to share your experiences with others who understand.

These spaces offer validation and reduce the feeling of isolation that can accompany trauma. Moreover, you have the power to shape the narrative. Your story, though born from pain, is ultimately a story of survival and resilience. Focusing on your strengths, the coping mechanisms you've developed, and the progress you've made allows you to highlight your inner strength and empowers you to tell your story on your terms. This isn't just about sharing your trauma; it's about sharing your triumph over adversity.

Consider the impact of your story by sharing your experiences, you can inspire others who have suffered in silence. Your vulnerability can help break down the stigma surrounding child abuse and create a more supportive environment for survivors. You can provide hope, reminding others that healing is possible and that they are not alone in their struggle. It's vital to recognise the potential challenges involved in sharing your story. You may experience difficult emotions as you revisit traumatic memories. It's crucial to have a strong support system in place to help you navigate these challenges. Allow yourself the time and space needed to process your feelings, and don't hesitate to seek professional help if you need it.

Remember, there will be days when sharing feels too difficult when the pain is overwhelming and that is 100% OK.

Be kind to yourself, respect your boundaries, acknowledge that progress and accept there will be setbacks along the way. Celebrate the small victories and remember the strength you've already shown in surviving.

Sharing your story allows you to reclaim your narrative, to shift from victim to survivor. It's a testament to your resilience, your courage, and your determination to heal. It's a gift not only to yourself but also to others who have suffered in silence.

Your voice deserves to be heard, and your story deserves to be shared.

The world needs to hear it.

The world needs your strength.

The world needs your hope.

Living a Full Life After Trauma Hope and Healing

For years, I believed my life was over before it had even begun. The cumulative weight of abuse, neglect, and the constant fight for survival left me feeling broken and irreparably damaged. The future stretched before me, a bleak and desolate landscape devoid of hope. I existed in a perpetual state of fight-or-flight, my nervous system perpetually on high alert, my mind a chaotic whirlwind of fragmented memories and suppressed emotions. Sleep offered little respite, haunted by nightmares that replayed the horrors I had endured. Even in waking hours, I felt a constant sense of unease, a deep-seated feeling that danger lurked around every corner.

The path to healing wasn't a straight line. It was more like navigating a treacherous mountain range, a winding, arduous journey fraught with setbacks, moments of doubt, and the persistent temptation to give up. There were times when I slipped, falling back into old patterns of self-destruction, retreating into the familiar darkness of isolation and despair. The shame lingered, a persistent shadow that threatened to consume me. I struggled to trust, to form healthy relationships, to believe that I deserved love and happiness. The memories, once suppressed, clawed their way back to the surface, assaulting me with their raw intensity.

Therapy was instrumental in helping me navigate this treacherous terrain. It provided a safe and supportive space where I could begin to process my trauma to give voice to my pain without judgment. My therapist, a compassionate and insightful man, helped me to understand the impact of my experiences and to develop healthy coping mechanisms. He taught me about the science of trauma, how it affects the brain and body, and how to begin to rewire those neural pathways that had been etched with fear and pain. He validated my experiences, reminding me that what I had endured was not my fault and that I was not alone. This was crucial; feeling heard and understood was a profound act of healing in itself.

Cognitive Behavioural Therapy (CBT) helped me challenge the negative and self-defeating thoughts that had become ingrained over the years. These thoughts were insidious, whispering insidious lies in my ear: "You're worthless," "You're unlovable," and "No one will ever truly care about you."

CBT provided me with the tools to identify and dispute these lies, replacing them with more positive and realistic ones. It was a painstaking process, a constant battle against ingrained patterns of thinking, but gradually, I began to see a shift in my perspective.

The negative self-talk became quieter and less insistent, and I started to believe in my own inherent worth.

Beyond therapy, I discovered the power of community. Connecting with other survivors, sharing our stories, and offering each other support was invaluable. It was in these spaces that I discovered I wasn't alone, that others had navigated similar paths, had emerged from the depths of despair, and were now living full and meaningful lives. This sense of shared experience, this solidarity in the face of adversity, was immensely empowering. It shattered the isolating shame that had held me captive for so long and gave me the courage to speak my truth.

The path to healing also involved confronting the physical manifestations of trauma. Years of suppressed emotions had taken a toll on my body, manifesting in chronic pain, digestive issues, and sleep disturbances. I began exploring various somatic therapies, including yoga, meditation, and body-centred psychotherapy. These practices helped me to connect with my body in a safe and nurturing way, to release pent-up tension and to cultivate a sense of self-awareness. The process was often uncomfortable, even painful, but it was also deeply liberating. I began to reclaim my body, to see it not as a vessel of trauma but as a source of strength and resilience.

I realised the importance of self-care. For years, I had neglected my own needs, putting everyone else's well-being before my own. Healing required me to prioritise my physical and emotional health. This included establishing healthy habits, engaging in regular exercise, getting enough sleep, and setting healthy boundaries. It meant saying no to things that depleted me and yes to activities that nourished my soul. Self-care was not a luxury; it was a necessity, a fundamental aspect of my recovery journey.

The journey toward living a full life after trauma is a lifelong commitment. It's not a destination you arrive at; rather, it's an ongoing process of growth, learning, and self-discovery. There will be moments of relapse, times when the old wounds reopen and the pain resurfaces. This is part of the process; it doesn't mean you've failed. It means you're human. The key is to approach these moments with self-compassion, recognising that they are temporary and that you have the strength and resilience to navigate them.

Today, I can say with conviction that a fulfilling life is possible after trauma. My past experiences have indelibly shaped me, leaving their mark on my life, but they do not define me. I am not simply a survivor; I am a testament to the extraordinary capacity of the human spirit to heal, to grow, and to thrive in the face of unimaginable adversity. I have learned that healing is not about forgetting; it is about integrating the past into a richer, more nuanced understanding of oneself. It is about embracing the lessons learned, utilising the wisdom gained, and transforming pain into purpose.

My story is not unique. Millions of people around the world have experienced childhood trauma, and countless others continue to suffer in silence. I share my story not for sympathy but to offer hope and encouragement to those who feel lost, broken, and alone. Know that you are not alone. Your story matters. Your pain is valid. And there is hope for healing and a path to living a full and meaningful life, a life beyond your trauma. Your resilience is greater than you know. Your capacity to heal is immense. Embrace the journey, even with its inevitable bumps and detours, and believe in the possibility of a brighter future. The path to healing is challenging, but the destination—a life filled with love, purpose, and joy—is worth the journey.

Healing is a winding road filled with unexpected turns and challenging terrain. There will be moments of intense pain and overwhelming emotion, setbacks and moments of doubt. It's perfectly okay to grieve the loss of the childhood you never had, the innocence that was stolen from you. Allow yourself to feel these emotions fully, without judgment or shame. Don't try to rush the process; healing takes time, patience, and self-compassion.

Seek out support. Don't try to navigate this journey alone. Connect with others who understand what you are going through – friends, family, support groups, or therapists. Sharing your story can be incredibly powerful, relieving the burden of carrying the weight of your experiences in silence. It helps you feel less isolated and reminds you that you are not alone in this struggle.

Forgive yourself. This is perhaps one of the most challenging aspects of the healing process. Forgiveness does not in any way mean you are condoning the actions of those who harmed you; it means releasing the self-blame and self-hatred that can perpetuate the cycle of trauma.

Forgiving yourself allows you to move forward, free from the shackles of self-criticism and self-doubt. It's a process, not a single event, and it will take time. Finally, remember your worth. You deserve to live a happy and fulfilling life. You deserve love, connection, and joy. Never forget that your experiences do not diminish your value. Your past does not dictate your future. You have the power to create the life you want, a life filled with purpose, meaning, and resilience.

Believe in yourself, embrace the hope of a brighter future.

The future is not defined by the past. It's a canvas on which you can paint your own masterpiece. Your strength, your courage, and your indomitable spirit will carry you through. You are a survivor. You are resilient, and you are worthy of a beautiful, fulfilling life.

Appendix

It is vital to remember that you are not alone, and help is available.

Australian Helplines
1800 RESPECT

1800 737 732 offers 24/7 support for people experiencing sexual assault, domestic violence, or family violence.

Kids Helpline 1800 551 800

Beyond Blue 1300 224 636

Bravehearts 1800 227 831

Lifeline 13 11 14

Police Link 13 14 44

United Kingdom Helplines

Action for Children

Provides national network of child sexual abuse treatment centres providing support and counselling for children and their families. Adult survivors also.

Chesham House, Church Lane, Berkhamstead, Herts HP4 2AX

Tel: 0300 123 2112

Website: www.actionforchildren.org.uk

SEREN

SEREN is a specialised counselling service in Wales for adults who have been sexually abused as children.

2nd Floor, NatWest Chambers, Sycamore Street, Newcastle Emlyn SA38 9AJ

Tel: 01239 711 772

Website: www.seren-wales.org.uk

London Lesbian and Gay Switchboard

Tel: 020 7837 7324; Monday to Sunday 10am-11pm

Website: www.llgs.org.uk

National Deaf Children's Society

Agency catering for deaf children and their families. Can offer books/information to professionals.

15 Dufferin Street, London EC1Y 8UR

Tel: 020 7490 8656, Helpline: 0808 800 8880 (also minicom); Monday to Friday 9.30 am-5 pm

Email: ndcs@ndcs.org.uk

Website: www.ndcs.org.uk

British Association for Counselling and Psychotherapy

BACP House, 15 St John's Business Park, Lutterworth LE17 4HB

Tel: 0870 443 5252 or 01455 883 300; Monday to Friday 8.45 am to 5 pm, both numbers

Email: bacp@bacp.co.uk

Website: www.bacp.co.uk

Clinical psychologists

Your GP can refer you to a clinical psychologist or you can ask another professional for advice on how to get to see a psychologist; or visit www.bps.org.uk, the website of the British Psychological Society.

United States of America Helplines

Childhelp National Child Abuse Hotline

www.childhelp.org

1-800-4ACHILD or 1-800-422-4453 | TDD: 1-800-2A-CHILD. 24/7 - Call from: USA, Canada, Puerto Rico, Guam or the Virgin Islands. - can help in 170 languages. All calls are confidential.

1800SUICIDE National Hopeline

www.hopeline.com

1.800.SUICIDE (784-2433) | Deaf + Hard of Hearing 1.800.799.4889 | En Español 1-888-628-9454 | Also: Help Chat Online

If you - or someone you know - are having thoughts about suicide, call 1.800.SUICIDE (784-2433). Calls are connected to a certified crisis center nearest the caller's location. Services are available 24 hours a day, seven days a week.

National Sexual Assault Hotline (RAINN) www.rainn.org

Get Help 24/7: 800.656.HOPE (4673) (English/Spanish) | or Live Chat | Many Resources on site.

Free. Confidential. 24/7.

After sexual assault, it's hard to know how to react. You may be physically hurt, emotionally drained, or unsure what to do next. You may be considering working with the criminal justice system, but are unsure of where to start. Learning more about what steps you can take following sexual violence can help ground you in a difficult time

GLBT Youth Talkline

www.glbthotline.org

GLBT Youth Talkline 1-800-246-PRIDE (1-800-246-7743) |

Gay, Lesbian, Bisexual and Transgender (GLBT) National Hotline 1-888-843-4564

Both hotlines operate Mon - Fri 4pm to midnight EST / Sat noon to 5pm EST)

Both hotlines provide telephone, online private one-to-one chat and email peer-support, as well as factual information and local resources for cities and towns across the United States.

Shalom Task Force national domestic abuse hotline

www.shalomtaskforce.org/hotline

"It hurts to call a domestic abuse hotline - It Hurts More Not To."

888-883-2323 or 718-337-3700 Collect Calls Accepted.

Yitti Leibel Helpline (Jewish)

New York City 1-718-HELP-NOW (435-7669)

Chicago 1-800-HELP-023

Lakewood, NJ 1-908-363-1010

Cleveland, OH 1-888-209-8079

Glossary

This glossary provides definitions for some key terms used throughout the book related to child abuse, trauma, and the healing process:

Childhood Trauma:

Experiences in childhood that significantly impact a person's emotional, psychological, and physical well-being, often leading to long-term effects.

Complex Trauma:

Prolonged or repeated exposure to trauma, particularly within the context of an ongoing relationship, such as child abuse.

Grooming:

The process by which an abuser manipulates and gains the trust of a victim, often a child, before committing abuse.

Intergenerational Trauma:

Trauma that is passed down from one generation to the next, impacting subsequent generations.

PTSD (Post-Traumatic Stress Disorder):

A mental health condition that can develop after experiencing or witnessing a terrifying event.

CPTSD (Complex Post-Traumatic Stress Disorder): A more complex form of PTSD, often stemming from prolonged or repeated trauma.

Trauma-Informed Care:

An approach to care that acknowledges the pervasive impact of trauma and seeks to create a safe and supportive environment for survivors.

LGBTQIA+:

This is an evolving acronym that stands for lesbian, gay, bisexual, transgender, intersex, queer/questioning, asexual. Many other terms such a non-binary and pansexual that people use to describe experiences of gender, sexuality and psychological sex characteristics.

Indigenous:

Indigenous Australian is a very general term that covers two distinctive cultural groups being Aboriginal and Torres Strait Islander peoples.

References

My memories, my life experiences, Google for support phone numbers.

SELF-HELP BOOKS FOR SURVIVORS

Ainscough, C. and Toon, K. (2000) Breaking Free: Help for Survivors of Child Sexual Abuse. London: Sheldon Press.

Sanford, L.T. (1990) Strong at the Broken Places: Overcoming the Trauma of Childhood Abuse. London: Virago.

FOR MALE SURVIVORS

Etherington, K. (1995) Adult Male Survivors of Sexual Abuse. London: Pitman Publishing.

Grubman-Black, S.D. (1990) Broken Boys/Mending Men: Recovery from Childhood Sexual Abuse. Blue Ridge Summit, PA: Tab Books.

Hunter, M. (1990) Abused Boys: The Neglected Victims of Sexual Abuse. Lexington, MA: Lexington.

Lew, M. (1988) Victims No Longer: Men Recovering from Incest and Other Sexual Child Abuse. New York: Neuramount Publishers.

FOR PARTNERS AND FAMILIES OF SURVIVORS

Davis, L. (1991) Allies in Healing: When the Person you Love was Sexually Abused as a Child. New York: Harper Perennial.

From Discovery to Recovery: A Parent's Survival Guide to Child Sexual Abuse.
Warwickshire Social Services department, PO Box 48, Shire Hall, Warwick CV34 4RD. Audiotape and booklet.

Bessel A. van der Kolk, M.D. (2014) The Body Keeps The Score: Brain, Mind, and Body in the Healing of Trauma.
ISBN 978-1-101-60830-2

Rothschild, B. (2000) The Body Remembers: The Psychophysiology of Trauma and Trauma Treatment. W. W. Norton & Company
ISBN 978-0-393-06868-9

Frank, G. Anderson, M.D (2021) Transcending-Trauma: Healing Complex PTSD with Internal Family Systems Therapy
ISBN 978-1-68373-397-3

Levine, P. (2010) In an Unspoken Voice: How the Body Releases Trauma and Restores Goodness

ISBN 978-1-58394-652-7

Sanderson, C. (2013) Counselling Skills for Working with Trauma: Healing From Child Sexual Abuse, Sexual Violence and Domestic Abuse.

SBN 978-1-84905-326-6

ISBN 978-0-85700-743-8

Winnette, P. and Baylin, J. (2017) Working with Traumatic Memories To Heal Adults With Unresolved Childhood Trauma: Neuroscience, Attachment Theory and Pesso Boyden System Psychomotor Psychotherapy

ISBN 978-1-84905-724-0

ISBN 978-1-78450-182-2

About the Author

Joe, the author of *Coming Out of the Dark*, is a survivor of childhood sexual abuse. After years of struggling with the profound impact of his trauma, he has embarked on a journey of healing and self-discovery. His experience led him to pursue a career in hospitality and property. He hopes to move across to social work, counselling, psychology or possibly nursing, where he plans to dedicate his life to supporting others.

He honestly believes in the power of sharing stories to break the cycle of silence and shame. He hopes this highly detailed book about his personal experiences with abuse and sexual abuse will offer hope, validation, and empowerment to others who have endured similar experiences. He currently resides in Brisbane, Australia, and truly hopes to continue assisting those that have gone through abuse in assisting them to find their survivor support and their voice to speak out and break the cycle of childhood sexual abuse.

A message to the abusers of the world—your victims, including children, may be silent now, but I assure you they will grow up, they will heal and they will find their voice.

They will NOT be silenced with shame, guilt, and fear.

www.ingramcontent.com/pod-product-compliance
Lightning Source LLC
Chambersburg PA
CBHW071728120626
46550CB00002B/430